10/7   12/7

900 Miles from Nowhere

900 Miles from Nowhere

STEVEN R. KINSELLA

MINNESOTA HISTORICAL SOCIETY PRESS

Voices from the Homestead Frontier

www.mhspress.org

The Minnesota Historical Society Press is a member of the Association of American University Presses.

Manufactured in the United States of America

10 9 8 7 6 5 4 3 2

♾ The paper used in this publication meets the minimum requirements of the American National Standard for Information Sciences —Permanence for Printed Library Materials, ANSI Z39.48–1984.

International Standard Book Numbers:
10-digit: 0–87351–572–2 (cloth)
13-digit: 978–0–87351–572–6 (cloth)

978
KIN H 11/1/06

Library of Congress
Cataloging-in-Publication Data

Kinsella, Steven R.
900 miles from nowhere :
    voices from the homestead frontier /
    Steven R. Kinsella.
      p.   cm.
Includes index.
ISBN-13: 978-0-87351-572-6
    (cloth : alk. paper)
ISBN-10: 0-87351-572-2
    (cloth : alk. paper)
  1. Frontier and pioneer life—
      Great Plains—Sources.
  2. Pioneers—Great Plains—
      Biography.
  3. Pioneers—Great Plains—Archives.
  4. Great Plains—Social life and
      customs—19th century—Sources.
  5. Great Plains—Social life and
      customs—20th century—Sources.
  6. Farm life—Great Plains—History—
      Sources.
  7. Community life—Great Plains—
      History—Sources.
  8. Great Plains—Biography.
  I. Title.
  II. Title: Nine hundred miles from
      nowhere.
F596.K584 2006
978—dc22   2006012639

For J A K
The great, great-grandson of homesteaders

900 Miles from Nowhere

Acknowledgments

This book would not have been possible without the assistance of the busy staffs of the Wyoming State Archives, the Denver Public Library, Augustana College, and the historical societies of Minnesota, Montana, South Dakota, North Dakota, Colorado, Nebraska, Kansas, Oklahoma, and Iowa. I am forever indebted to them for their knowledge, support, and assistance.

I am also beholden to my family for their patience during my many absences as I repeatedly ventured across the Great Plains; to Alicka Pistek, of the Alicka Pistek Literary Agency, for her unwavering belief in this project; to the Minnesota Historical Society and especially to Marilyn Ziebarth, for her editing skills and sensitivity to the letters and diary entries; and to all the others, too numerous to mention, who helped me along the way. Finally, to those who, for whatever reasons, had the foresight to save these letters and diaries, thank you.

Prologue

One summer while attending college, I worked as a member of an archaeological field survey team, mapping historic and prehistoric sites along the James River in southeastern South Dakota. Walking along the bottomlands of a small tributary on a hot July day, we came across an odd-looking building entwined in trees and undergrowth. We discovered as we approached that it was a small, deteriorating sod house.

In history classes I had read about sod houses—the home of choice for many early settlers. I had learned about homesteaders and pioneers and read the works of writers like Laura Ingalls Wilder, Willa Cather, and O. E. Rølvaag. Yet I had never actually seen or experienced a real sod house. When we walked into the crumbling structure, before us lay the partially preserved life of a Great Plains pioneer: a rusted iron bed with a mouse-eaten mattress; a dilapidated dresser, its drawers stacked with old, stained clothing; a broken handmade table and chairs; mail-order catalogs swollen to twice their original size from snow and rain that had blown through the open door and broken windows; tattered remnants of lace curtains; and, most amazing of all, worn shelves with rows of canning jars, whose once promising sustenance grown in the soils of the Great Plains long ago had turned dark and clouded.

We stood silent; we felt as though we were amid spirits. Normally, our routine would have been simply to record a site on a topographical map, take a few pictures, and then move on. But that day we lingered. We walked in and out and around the building, saying little to each other, our attention absorbed by the house, its contents, and, most of all, by questions. Who had lived in this simple structure of grass and earth? Whose personal possessions did we hold in our hands? This experience has never left me.

The sight of abandoned farmhouses has always haunted me. Growing up on the northern Great Plains, I observed them as a child during family car trips across South Dakota and North Dakota. Struck by the ghostly, weathered appearance of a house, I often wondered if children like me had once lived there and, if so, what had happened to them.

As I grew older, these deserted buildings continued to affect me. Whether I was driving on the southern Great Plains through Oklahoma and Kansas or on the western reaches in Colorado and Montana, such forsaken structures were always a part of the landscape. Some had been built in the late 1800s, others in the early twentieth century, and a few as recently as the 1940s. Although the houses differed in size and style, they all bore a striking resemblance. They were tired and worn, their windows long gone. Rusted farm machinery and a couple of small, deteriorating outbuildings usually surrounded them. A few hand-planted trees, commonly referred to as windbreaks or shelterbelts, flanked them, at one time placed in neat rows around the house and outbuildings. Most striking of all, the farmhouses looked as though their existence had been interrupted. These homes had not been abandoned for larger, newer farmhouses down the road. These homes had been intentionally left behind, along with the hopes and aspirations of the families.

Several summers ago, I was traveling by car from my home in St. Paul, Minnesota, to the Black Hills of South Dakota and Wyoming. Once again the sight of these desolate buildings moved me, especially in western South Dakota, where the expansive sky and sweeping plains of grass dwarf the structures. During that trip I decided I would compile the thoughts and experiences of the inhabitants of these farm and ranch houses. I would collect their stories, in their own words, to tell what it was like to live in houses made of sod or tar paper and boards. Why had they come? How did it feel to be surrounded by grass for as far as the eye could see? What was it like to confront the enormous challenges presented by weather and grasshoppers? And why did so many leave? Perhaps their stories would answer these questions.

During the next few years, I spent countless hours in historical society archives, museums, and libraries, poring over manuscript collections and reading the letters, diaries, and remembrances of early non-Indian settlers. I looked at thousands of photographs, many fragile and carefully placed in photo albums nearly a century before. My original intention was to compile excerpts from the letters and diaries. I quickly discovered that while I could do this with diaries, the letters were far too rich in experiences and character to edit down to a few sentences.

Along the way, I learned about my own family and their experiences on the Great Plains. I had always heard my father's family described as "North Dakota farmers." After looking closely at a family history written by my cousin and my father, however, I discovered my grandparents were homesteaders. These first- and second-generation Irish immigrants, whose ancestors had fled famine, sold their small successful farms on the edge of the Great Plains in southeastern Minnesota and moved onto 160-acre homesteads on the fabled wheat fields of northwestern North Dakota. Living in roughly built claim shacks, they suffered through blizzards in the winter and scorching heat and drought in the summer. They struggled to farm inhospitable land. They made money in the good years and fell into debt in the bad ones. Eventually, unable to eke out a living, they were forced to abandon their farms.

I also discovered how the experiences of settlers in the region shaped not only the lives of the people I grew up with but also the character of America itself. Dwellers on the Great Plains today exhibit a fiercely guarded independence, yet they rarely have to be asked to help people in need, even strangers. They just do it. This is a trait born out of generations spent living on an often lonely and harsh land, where economic and human survival depends on community spirit and neighborliness.

At times, as I read the settlers' letters and diaries—including many touched by human hands less than a half-dozen times in the past century—I felt as though I were intruding. Some letters were deeply personal, especially those written by people who had been forced to ask for financial assistance, plead for food, and even beg for help in providing underclothing for their children. What kept me going was the image of those farmhouses, emptied of their dreams, that most passersby might see as little more than ordinary features of the landscape, like rocks, trees, or billboards.

This book's plaintive title, *900 Miles from Nowhere*, comes from a letter by a new bride whose husband had just taken her to a sod house in western South Dakota. The letters and diary entries—edited only lightly for clarity and comprehension—are much more than just a collection of such personal documents. They chronicle the spirit of a sturdy and determined people who sought to better their lives on the harsh, inhospitable landscape of the Great Plains. Their battle to prove themselves added a stirring chapter of struggle and resilience to the story of the United States.

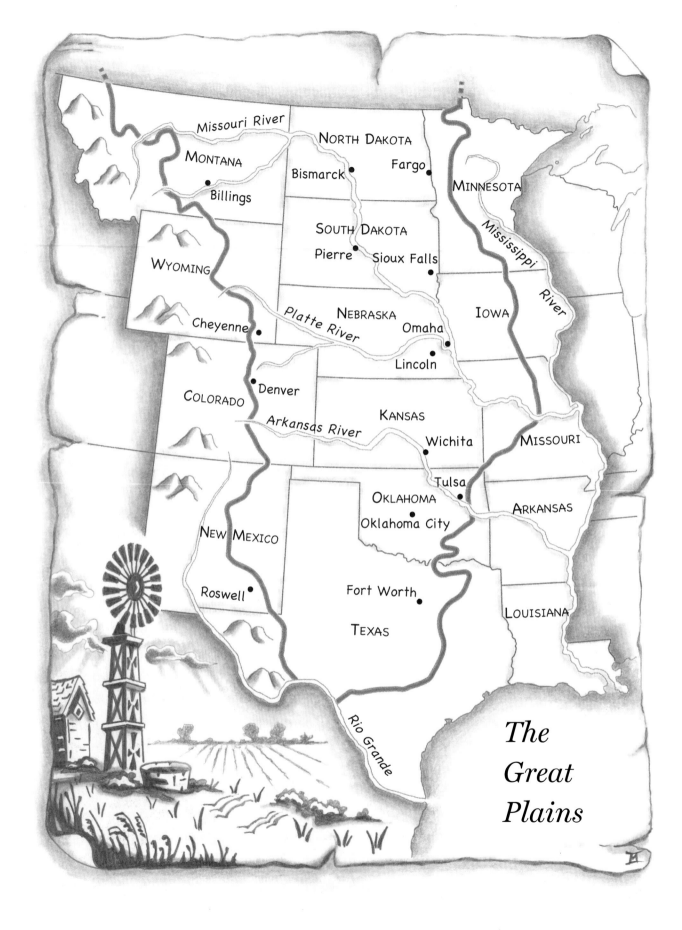

Missouri River

NORTH DAKOTA

MONTANA

Bismarck

Fargo

Billings

MINNESOTA

SOUTH DAKOTA

Pierre

Sioux Falls

Mississippi River

WYOMING

NEBRASKA

IOWA

Cheyenne

Platte River

Omaha

Lincoln

Denver

COLORADO

Arkansas River

KANSAS

Wichita

MISSOURI

Tulsa

OKLAHOMA

ARKANSAS

Oklahoma City

NEW MEXICO

Roswell

Fort Worth

LOUISIANA

TEXAS

Rio Grande

The Great Plains

900 Miles from Nowhere

*South Dakota's immigration commissioner sponsored this poster
advertising the virtues of free and cheap lands in the state.*

Introduction to the Great Plains

THE GREAT PLAINS. The words fail to suggest the imprint this land made on America's history and character. Here, amid the vast grassland and engulfing sky, people from around the world settled in search of the personal and economic freedom represented by land ownership. Traveling across continents and oceans, they arrived with shovels and plows and stood on their piece of America, believing they were part of something bigger. They were. Through hardships and triumphs, they developed the core of the American continent, a region once thought of as uninhabitable, and in doing so helped to shape the nation's sense of determination and independence.

Yet the effort came at a high cost. Inclement weather and the economic challenges of farming meant that far more settlers failed than were successful. Native Americans were pushed off their lands and herded onto reservations, many of which were later parceled off to feed an unquenchable desire for land. Once exposed by plowing, fragile prairie soil held intact over eons by rooted grass blew away in the winds. Today, the story of Great Plains settlement continues to unfold as inhabitants struggle with many of the same forces faced by those who arrived more than one hundred years ago.

Stretching from Texas through the central United States and into Canada, the vast expanse known as the Great Plains encompasses about one million square miles. To sense its scale, you need only drive through portions of central Kansas, Oklahoma, the Dakotas, or eastern Montana, where you will see an uninterrupted flat or rolling landscape extending for fifteen miles in any direction. Growing up there, I heard stories of inner-city youth sent out for summer work programs on the reservations who were made uneasy by the immensity—especially at night. Standing alone on the Great Plains gives people a sense of being minute and insignificant. The plains have humbled mankind ever since humans first set foot on them more than twelve thousand years ago.[1]

Far from uniform, the Great Plains are home to radically diverse landscapes. On the west they are bordered by the spiny slope of the Rocky Mountains. The Great Plains' eastern border runs roughly through Minnesota, Iowa, Missouri, Oklahoma, and Texas. Within these boundaries are the Black Hills (claiming the highest elevation found between the Rocky Mountains and the Atlantic Ocean), the Badlands of South and North Dakota, the stark, rolling Sandhills of Nebraska, and fertile river valleys like the Missouri, the Platte, and the Arkansas.

The greater part of the Great Plains, however, was and still is a treeless prairie. This is why, when asked to use one word to describe the region, people passing through and residents alike will settle on words like "flat" and "desolate" and "boring." Observer Ian Frazier, in *The Great Plains*, describes western Nebraska as "a land of grassy rises receding into the distance like a sea in a heavy chop."[2]

When my friends and I were first learning to drive, we traversed the dusty gravel roads outside my hometown of Mitchell, South Dakota, often in the truck or car of a farmer's son, licensed at age fourteen so he could drive himself to school. We followed unplanned, circuitous routes, spending hours driving hundreds of miles on the one-mile-square checkerboard pattern of roads. We knew we would never get seriously lost. We had only to drive a few miles in any direction, and a town's water tower or grain elevators would appear on the horizon, giving us our bearings.

The physical characteristics of the Great Plains were shaped by geologic and climatic forces. A shallow sea once covered them, eventually drying up and leaving behind thousands of feet of sediment. Later, the uplifting of the Rocky Mountains and the erosion that followed caused even more sediment to flow onto the plains. Glaciers also helped sculpt the surface and create the river basins. Over millions of years, these forces created a flat and rolling expanse of fertile soils that produced vibrant tall- and short-grass prairies.[3]

For centuries, the Great Plains were home to nomadic Indian tribes such as the Cheyenne, Lakota, and Kiowa, who hunted the animals that thrived there, and the Mandan, who farmed near its rivers and streams. Although early French explorers, trappers, and fur traders had explored and lived on the plains, the area was one of the last in the United States to be settled by non-Indians. Lieutenant Zebulon Pike, a U.S. government explorer who journeyed through the region in 1806 and 1807, wrote in his journals that the vast plains were comparable to the "desarts" of Africa and that they would restrict the expansion of the young nation. In 1820 Major Stephen H. Long, an officer with the U.S. Corps of Topographical Engineers who was mapping the region, coined the pejorative phrase "The Great American Desert" to describe the plains because of their lack of trees and semiaridity.[4]

The Great Plains—save for the river bottoms and mountainous regions such as the Black Hills—were treeless for a reason. Trees, much more than grass, need water to survive. At least one-half of the region receives twenty inches or less of rain and snow annually; portions receive a paltry sixteen inches or less per year. (In comparison, Pennsylvania has an average annual precipitation of 42 inches.) Prairie fires often burned off the few trees that did attempt to grow.[5]

The grasses that typically covered the plains reflected the rainfall levels. To the east settlers found lush tall-grass prairie with varieties such as big bluestem that can grow over six feet in height. In the central regions west of the ninety-eighth meridian, where average precipitation drops to twenty inches or less, were grasses such as little bluestem and wheat grass that grow to three feet. In the far western reaches with the least precipitation, ankle-high strains such as buffalo and grama grass were common.

While the climate of the region was good for the animals and peoples who understood and depended on the prairie, observers living elsewhere in the United States during the early and mid-1800s viewed the region as little more than an area to be passed through with haste. Its isolation and semiarid qualities, coupled with powerful and territorially possessive Indian tribes, diminished the region's value to the young nation. Some early explorers went so far as to claim that the Great Plains were "incapable of cultivation." By the 1840s, maps and textbooks printed in the United States had helped to cement this belief by labeling the region with Long's phrase, "The Great American Desert."[6]

Ironically, at the same time that these maps and textbooks were circulating, the rapidly growing nation was moving inland. Westward routes, including the Mormon Trail and others leading to Oregon and California, crossed the Great Plains, leaving scattered settlements in their wake. In the 1830s and 1840s, settlers began establishing farms and towns in Iowa and Minnesota. By the 1860s, the flow of settlers had reached western Missouri, Kansas, Nebraska, and even the Dakotas, as people began to take advantage of the opening of lands once reserved to Indians.

Creating another incentive for settling was the Preemption Act, which permitted the government to sell surveyed and unsurveyed tracts of land in the vast interior of the nation to squatters or settlers. The act went through a number of variations after its inception in the early 1800s, but under the act of 1841, preempters who located a home on 160 acres and improved the land could buy it for $1.25 an acre after living on the land for a minimum of six months.[7]

The easy terms of the Preemption Act also attracted land speculators and investors who used it as a quick way to make money. The conditions were so lax that many speculators filed claims under the act, held on to the land for the required number of months, often making questionable improvements to the property, and then sold it or turned it over to the mortgage holder.[8]

While several economic factors briefly slowed migration onto the Great Plains—the nation's entry into the Civil War in 1861, increased hostilities by Indian tribes against settlers, and the decline of railroad construction—the demand for free land continued. Accordingly, in 1862 Congress passed what became known as the Homestead Act. Unlike the Preemption Act, which required that land be purchased, the Homestead Act simply gave away up to 160 acres of land for free. In exchange, settlers agreed to pay a small filing fee and live on the land for five years while making improvements. This was known as "proving up" or "making proof" on the claim. (Settlers also had the option of living on the homestead claim for six months, making improvements, and then purchasing the land for $1.25 per acre, or $2.50 per acre if it was within a railroad right-of-way. Minimum residency was later extended to fourteen months.) Excluded from

Government surveying parties, including this crew working in Oklahoma Territory in 1893, divided the Great Plains into townships, sections, and quarter sections.

the act were married women (unless they could prove they were heads of households) and American Indians, a group barred from citizenship.[9]

In the mid-1860s, migration onto the Great Plains exploded. Settlers took advantage of the Homestead and Preemption options, the end of the Civil War, wide-scale railroad construction, and treaties forced on Indian tribes. A revised Homestead Act gave preferential treatment to Union veterans and their widows and orphans by applying years in military service to the residency requirement. Other congressional land acts, such as the Timber Culture Act of 1873 (which gave away free land for planting trees on the prairie) and the Enlarged Homestead Act of 1909 (which increased the free land allotment to 320 acres in drier regions), enticed further settlement.

With Uncle Sam willing to give a free farm to anyone who wanted it, people throughout the world took notice. It mattered not who you were, what language you spoke, your religion or ethnic background, or the social status of your family; all you had to do was find your way to the Great Plains, where a promising future awaited you. Union Civil War veterans, adventurers, seekers of wealth and status, college graduates, freed slaves, newlyweds, Europe's economically and socially downtrodden, speculators, extended families, and single women all seized on the opportunity to share in the wealth and bounty of America's land. (The first homestead claim was reportedly filed within minutes after the Homestead Act became law near Beatrice, Nebraska.)[10]

Encouraged onward by railroad and shipping line posters proclaiming "Free Land," the hopeful—referred to as "homesteaders," "boomers," "sodbusters," "honyockers," and "dry farmers"—flooded in to fulfill their dreams. Promoters and homesteaders themselves even created colonies to help groups relocate together, such as the African American colony of Nicodemus, Kansas.

In the mid-1800s, many of the settlers came from nearby states like Illinois, Wisconsin, and Iowa, but as time passed, more and more arrived from around the globe. In the second half of the nineteenth century, the world was still largely an agriculture-based society, and land ownership signified prosperity and social status. Free or cheap land under the Homestead and Preemption acts opened doors of promise for Europeans, including Russians, who had endured generations of poverty, and Scandinavians, who lived under a system in which only oldest sons could inherit land. Millions of Norwegians, Swedes, Finns, Irish, English, Scots, Germans (including ethnic Germans residing in Russia), Dutch, Czechs, and religious minorities such as Mennonites and Hutterites flowed onto the prairies in search of economic opportunities. Today, the legacy of this great transport of people from throughout the world may be seen on state maps filled with place names such as Strasburg, Gothenburg, Frankfort, and

Tabor and in the foods, customs, and traditions common to these cultural enclaves.[11]

New settlers were further enticed by the systematic efforts of railroads and territorial and state promoters to ease doubts over adequate moisture. The long-held belief that the Great Plains were a desert inhospitable to growing crops was countered at large exhibitions and fairs in the eastern United States and in touring railroad cars showing the agricultural potential of the region. They heralded new agricultural theories and farming practices, detailing how the prairie could be successfully farmed. An optimistic theory—"Rain follows the plow"—promoted the belief that as more people broke the sod and released moisture into the atmosphere, rainfall would increase in the region.[12]

Little stood in the way of these promotional efforts—including the truth. A typical 1885 publication titled *Dakota—Behold, I Show You a Delightsome Land* noted, "This little book is designed to tell the truth about Dakota" and asserted that information contained in the book was "vouched for as correct by duly constituted officials." In the section on issues facing would-be settlers, the author answered the question, "Is it true that Dakota farmers are frequent sufferers from drought?" with the response, "It is not true." The author further explained that while there was less moisture than in some of the eastern regions of the United States, the rainfalls in Dakota occurred "just when they are needed most."[13]

While the offer of free land in a crop-growing area provided an incentive for people to move in, the resumption of railroad construction on a broad scale after the Civil War made such a move economically feasible—at least in concept. Settlers became convinced that no matter how far into the Great Plains they moved, the railroads would soon follow, as would towns and then cities. Local and national markets would be created for their crops and livestock, turning their initial hard work into a money-making venture. This would in turn rapidly increase the value of their land.[14]

The railroads had their own financial stake in increasing settlement. In addition to the profit potential of hauling freight and people in and out of an agricultural region, railroads had as an extra incentive the U.S. government's offer of right-of-way concessions. Railroads were generously given free title to as much as one-half of the land twenty miles deep on either side of their tracks. Railroads could create towns and sell town lots or break up the parcels into farmable quarter sections for sale to settlers arriving to make the plains their home.[15]

Those who had come to farm and build new lives on the prairies weren't the only ones showing up. Land speculators—sometimes referred to as "six and fourteen month men"—came to live on their farms for the minimum time period required by the law and then sold them for a profit. There were land locators, often former government land surveyors who had platted the region into townships, sections, and quarter sections and who, for a fee, would show "choice" settlement and homestead sites. Merchants and lawyers also found their way onto the Great Plains, quickly followed by bankers and mortgage lenders, all of whom flocked to towns created to serve those engaged in agriculture. Many of the early settlers had arrived almost penniless, having used their limited resources to get to the Great Plains and buy the few provisions necessary to survive the first year. Early financiers were more than willing to provide money in the form of a mortgage lien against the land, often with exorbitant interest rates.[16]

The human tide of settlers flowed and ebbed as people moved onto the plains, at times so rapidly that they staked out claims ahead of the government survey teams platting the land. On occasion, they backtracked to areas previously bypassed by the railroads or moved to take advantage of Indian reservation parcels that had been broken up to meet the demand for land. The pace of the non-Indian settlement of the Great Plains was

The Northern Pacific encouraged settlement of the Great Plains with this traveling display of products harvested on former railroad lands, 1895.

extraordinary by any standard. When it ended in the second decade of the twentieth century, an area that had once been a "sea of grass"—a mass of land one million square miles in size—was filled with cities and towns, a transportation infrastructure of railroads and roads, hundreds of thousands of farms and ranches, and millions of people. The population of North Dakota alone grew from an estimated 16,000 in 1878 to 191,000 in 1890. Most settlers were foreign born or the children of immigrants. A second boom brought on by increasing land values saw the population of that state grow by an additional 81 percent, to 577,000, in the period between 1900 and 1910. In Montana, homesteaders were registering land claims at the staggering rate of between 1,000 and 1,500 per month in 1910. A single land lottery for homesteads in South Dakota in July 1904 had more than 106,000 applicants filing for only 2,412 land claims.[17]

Standing on their new farms, or in their newly platted towns, and staring out across the treeless landscape, the settlers—especially the wiser among them—must have recognized that the land had the potential to stare back. Although they had come from across the nation or around the world in search of wealth, status, and freedom, what they found, more often than not, was a land unreceptive to the farming practices of the time. As the early explorers recognized, the Great Plains were better known for long droughts, fierce blizzards, tornadoes, subzero temperatures, grasshopper plagues, and prairie fires than for producing agricultural bounties.

And though the prairie could be stunningly beautiful, especially in the spring, there existed very few contemporary conveniences, especially for people living in the formerly unsettled reaches. There were no roads to speak of. Post offices could be more than a day's journey away and railroads were often several days or weeks away. There were no schools or churches, or the sense of community they bring. No doctors or hospitals. No readily accessible building materials and household goods. Few trees, if any, for shade or lumber or fencing. Little or no surface water. Not many neighbors.

In spite of these challenges, the settlers—many of whom had never farmed a day in their lives—dug in, rolled up their sleeves, and tried to tough it out, building houses of sod or shacks made of little more than tar paper and boards. They planted gardens, plowed the virgin prairie, and dug wells or hauled water from nearby streams or sloughs. When it rained, when nature cooperated, and when the price of agricultural commodities was high, life was good. The settlers made money, expanded their farms and businesses, bought more livestock and luxuries like parlor organs or pianos, and built frame houses. But when things turned bad, life became hard. Droughts shriveled up crops, often accompanied by massive clouds of grasshoppers that descended from the skies. Blizzards, tornadoes, grassfires, and widespread disease compounded the settlers' sense of isolation and loneliness. Uncertain agricultural prices sometimes meant that they didn't even make enough money to cover the cost of planting their crops.

With every period of environmental and economic catastrophe, some settlers on the Great Plains fled for lives elsewhere, their homes and possessions sold or abandoned. But, like hopeless romantics, as soon as a drought cycle ended and the rains resumed or farm prices increased again, other families replaced them. They often bought the farms of those who had failed or, with unfettered optimism, staked out their own claims farther west, where rainfall levels were even lower.

Promoters did all they could to downplay the out-migration. A pamphlet published by the Chicago, Milwaukee and St. Paul Railway titled *Dakota, the Land of Promise—How to Go and What to Do When You Get There* claimed the departure of these people had nothing to do with the inhospitality of the region. It said the abandoned farms were caused solely by restlessness. Furthermore, it associated these settlers with Indians, which at the time meant their behavior would be held in question. "There are a certain class of settlers occupying public lands known as 'pioneers.' They are as restless as the Indian and usually follow in his footsteps. They want plenty of room and cannot tolerate the confinement of boundaries produced by new neighbors. . . . Anticipating the natural tendencies of this class of settlers, the government has so amended the land laws as to permit of the abandonment of their claims, thus letting the land revert back to the government, and simultaneously allowing any other qualified settler to file a claim on it."[18]

Growing awareness of the difficulty of homesteading in semiarid country induced Congress to pass the Enlarged Homestead Act in 1909, providing homesteaders in drier states with 320 acres, instead of the 160 acres made available under the original act. By then, however, the terms "dry" and "drought" were so poisonous that the State of South Dakota chose not to participate in the Enlarged Homestead Act, at least until 1915, for fear of being viewed as one of the dry states. For many living on the western reaches of the Great Plains, even 320 acres was not enough land to survive on.[19]

During hard times, the settlers did all they could to survive, hanging on in whatever way possible, living in fear of a visit from the mortgage holder or the owner of the farm equipment note. Some found other jobs to supplement the subsistence of farming or ranching, and some just left, chewed up and spit out by the Great Plains. While many held on and survived, most of the first-time settlers did not. Many did not even make it to the five-year mark when a homestead claim was "proved up" and theirs for the taking. By the early years of the twentieth century, some regions had already lost as much as half of their population.[20]

Those who did survive did so with grit and unimaginable determina-

European immigrants crowded on board a ship bound for the United States, about 1890

tion. Many were European and Russian immigrants who had endured generations of poverty and were psychologically better equipped to live through the hard times the region was capable of delivering. Others were the second or third owners of a homestead, preemption, or railroad claim, whose purchase coincided with a run of favorable weather and commodity prices, which allowed them to build up the farm's production value and equity. Some were simply too poor to leave and eked out an existence hoping and praying for better times.[21]

The creation of newer and more efficient farm machinery enabled a number of settlers to hang on. So did periods of highly favorable commodity prices and technologies like irrigation, which were used with mixed success to combat Mother Nature's fickleness. To help their farm or ranch produce a larger and more diverse volume of agricultural products, thereby making it more economical in times of fluctuating commodity prices, some settlers bought additional land, including the homesteads of those who left. In many cases, especially on the western plains, land that had been broken for the purpose of raising crops was put back to grass for the production of cattle or sheep.

Still others, like my great-grandparents, were able to make a living farming on the Great Plains until the 1930s, when yet another drought, coupled with the Great Depression, finally broke the back of their homestead. After they lost their farm to creditors, my great-grandparents spent the rest of their lives living in a small house in nearby Northgate, North Dakota, their parlor organ and Studebaker the only reminder of a time when life had been good on the farm.

Through all these years and troubles, from the beginnings of the non-Indian settlement on the Great Plains in the mid-1800s to its end in the second decade of the twentieth century, settlers wrote home whenever they could. Using ink quills, pencils, and, later, typewriters, they excitedly described the majestic beauty of the prairie. Corresponding with friends and family back east or in their European homelands, they encouraged them to come and stake out a farm for themselves. They chronicled their excitement and pride when they filed their claim, their struggles attempting to tame the land agriculturally, and their disappointment and pain when the farm failed to produce the expected crop or produced nothing at all. They also filled diaries and journals with thoughts and impressions of their journey and their daily experiences on the land. Diaries became outlets for lonely settlers with no one else to talk to.

Occasionally, a single letter turned into a running, multiday rumination. Letter-writing settlers communicated frequently or infrequently with friends, family, acquaintances, and business associates from afar. Isolation on the prairie increased the value of letters. So significant was the prospect of receiving a letter that some rode a horse for hours after a day of hard work to reach a post office. If no letter was there, they would ride back to the farm, only to repeat the trip the next day and the next if necessary. Many settlers kept careful logs of each letter sent and received, and a common refrain in their letters was that the recipient "owed" them a letter.

These letters were equally important to those who received them. The correspondence often came from children whom parents would never see or talk to again. For some, the Great Plains were an exotic place, and the letter recipients hungered for information about life there. Still others wanted detailed information on the challenges of farming on the prairie so they could decide whether or not to pull up roots and establish their own farms there.

Letters and diary entries frequently focused on two themes—the weather and the crops—especially if the author was engaged in agriculture. These factors were key to their economic well-being and affected the always-uncertain future. Even today, the obsession with these two topics continues. If you want to start a conversation anywhere on the Great Plains, you only need ask, "How's the weather been?" or "Have you gotten much rain this summer?" or "How are your crops doing?" The questions serve as sure icebreakers, instantly telling the listener that no matter where you may be from or what your background is, you know what is important and worth talking about.

The saga of the Great Plains settlers continues to this day. The fierce independence of the people who live there, their survival instincts, their suspicion of outsiders, and their contempt for some government institutions and private conglomerates, like railroads, grain companies, and banks, all have their roots in the settlement era. Throughout the region there is a particular distaste for those who make money on investments and the hard work of farmers or ranchers. People in the business of agriculture know what it feels like to assume the lion's share of the risk and the cost of failure. North Dakota still has a state-owned bank and a system of state-owned grain elevators established in 1919. Farmers there began the socialist experiment when they became fed up with their treatment by out-of-state banks and the dishonest policies of grain companies when it came to grading and paying for crops.

The struggle to survive in a land inhospitable to agriculture is also ongoing. Some regions on the Great Plains reached their peak population levels around the turn of the past century and have lost inhabitants since then. Positive economic trends existing in the rest of the nation bypassed many areas due to their nearly exclusive dependence on agriculture. According to the 2000 census, 272 of 443 counties on the Great Plains have lost population since 1990. In some locations, the prairie is reclaiming its hold on the terrain, a frank commentary by nature. Contrary to human be-

Settlers mailing letters from a tent post office in Guthrie, Oklahoma Territory, 1889

lief, technology and enterprising settlers could not readily tame the land into tidy plots of cultivated crops.[22]

For better or worse, the agricultural policies of the United States—and the world, due to our global dominance in agricultural trade—are an outgrowth of what occurred on the Great Plains. Agriculture price supports, disaster payments, and complex farm programs all have their roots in the fickle nature of the region and the difficulties that small, independent farmers and ranchers have had trying to make a living there. Not surprisingly, that dependency nags at Great Plains residents—people who have held aloft the notion of self-determination since the beginning. In 1993, when I was selected to serve as the press secretary to the U.S. secretary of agriculture, a fairly haughty appointment for a small-town boy from South Dakota, many of my farm and ranch friends rolled their eyes. It wasn't that they weren't proud of me—they were—they just didn't like where I was going to work.

When nature cooperates, agricultural production is bountiful in the Great Plains. While 160-acre farmsteads have become relics, larger farms and ranches produce an abundance of agricultural commodities that feed much of the United States—and the world, for that matter. Kansas alone produces one-fifth of the wheat grown in the United States—roughly 374 million bushels annually. North Dakota, Montana, South Dakota, and Minnesota lead the world in the production of durum and hard red spring wheat—the two preferred varieties for pasta and flour. Six of the top ten corn-producing states and four of the top five oat-producing states are also located there.

The Great Plains are a place of great contradictions. In spite of a general dislike of government and certain elements of the free-enterprise system, residents hold an unwavering belief in democracy and the economic and political freedoms it represents. In the 2004 election, Great Plains states made up half of the sixteen states with the highest percentage of eligible voters who voted. This reflects the nature of the individuals who settled there, many of whose descendants live there today. These settlers, some of whom voted for the first time in their lives when they came to the United States, risked everything for the privilege of owning land. They instilled in their children and grandchildren a deep-seated belief in the responsibilities of citizenship, the privilege of living in a democracy, and the importance of protecting those freedoms.

So, too, despite the independent nature of the people, there is a profound sense of community on the Great Plains. Surveys conducted by the Bureau of Business and Economic Research at the University of Montana record that a large number of people stay there, in spite of the challenges they face, because of family, friends, and neighbors. The findings make sense when you consider that this is a place where economic and sometimes even human survival have often meant relying on those networks. Not surprisingly, similar surveys of urban residents have found that jobs are what keep them where they are.[23]

The images associated with those who settled on the Great Plains have left an impression on all Americans. Marketers today sell cars, clothes, food, and political candidates by plucking the heartstrings of American consumers with images of ranchers, farmers, and rural town dwellers exuding wholesome, patriotic, and independent values. To demonstrate the wealth of the nation, advertisers show amber waves of grain being harvested by a solitary man in a tractor, not suit-and-tie traders on Wall Street.

In *The Middle West—Its Meaning in American Culture*, James Shortridge notes that the region provides the nation with a "touchstone" for what it sees as its positive values and has become a metaphor for all that Americans believe to be good about their character. This notion—based in myth and fact—is an outgrowth, in large part, of images associated with settlement of the Great Plains and the tenacity of people who survived there. Americans want to believe that humankind, through technology, hard work, and personal resolve, can conquer everything, including nature. The Great Plains tests those beliefs but cannot diminish the efforts of the men and women, successful or not, who attempted to settle them.[24]

Today, America is a better and richer place thanks to the hardy souls who packed up everything they owned and crossed oceans and prairies to better their lot, facing adversity and immeasurable personal challenges. These settlers enhanced our cultural diversity, our sense of independence, our tenacity, and the vigor of our political institutions. The United States is a stronger and more confident nation because of them.

A patriotic farmer riding a sulky plow, 1910s

A family with horses, cows, and wagons seeking land in Nebraska

Toward the Setting Sun

The earliest homesteaders and settlers traveled to the Great Plains most often in large canvas-covered wagons—sometimes referred to as prairie schooners. The wagons were pulled by teams of oxen, horses, or mules that would later be put to work dragging plows and other pieces of farm equipment. Wagons often served as temporary homes once homesteaders arrived at their destination. Many went as far as they could by train or boated up rivers like the Missouri—and then transferred to wagons, carriages, or buggies. Still others rode on horseback and some even walked. As railroads laid track farther and farther westward, access became easier. By the late 1800s and early 1900s, those traveling to the western areas of the Great Plains could simply ride a train into the region and then go in search of the farm or town where they might settle.

The trips took anywhere from days to months, depending on where they originated and whether they were made in the middle of the nineteenth century or the beginning of the twentieth century. The journeys were not only long—they were difficult and dangerous. Wagons frequently broke down and horses sometimes stampeded off into the plains. Pets and even small children could wander off and get lost in the tall-grass prairies. Illness and death along the trail were common. Rain, snow, hail, lightning, tornadoes, and fires appeared suddenly, leaving settlers out in the open without shelter. Highwaymen, taking advantage of the vulnerability of travelers, robbed and even killed them. American Indians, resentful of the intrusion into their lands, harassed and sometimes attacked them. During the Civil War era, border ruffians threatened, harassed, and killed settlers who favored Kansas as a slavery-free state.

Like the ancient mariners, those journeying in search of land and new homes used the stars at night to determine their bearings. A number of the trails across the Great Plains had been forged by American Indians centuries before and followed the path of least resistance, having fewer obstacles like sloughs and ravines and easier river crossings. Seeing the advantage of these routes, latter-day highway planners and engineers graveled and then paved them, creating many of the highways and interstates that crisscross the region today.

When settlers arrived at their destination, they went about finding a home in one of several ways. Going to the nearest government land office in the area they wanted to settle, they obtained plat maps showing townships, sections, and unclaimed quarter sections of land and then wandered the countryside in search of their 160-acre claim. They might seek several claims, if friends or family members were settling together, or if an individual was using a combination of the Homestead, Timber Culture, or Preemption land acts. Others hired one of the many land locators whose offices sprang up almost as quickly as the small towns that were being established in the settlers' wake. For a fee, the land locators would show them prime quarters of government, railroad, or private land that were available. Those with adequate resources bought farms from those who had successfully proved up their claims and had then decided to sell, either to make a profit or because life on the prairie proved too much for them.[25]

So important was the act of claiming a piece of land that the term has become part of our everyday speech. While today the phrase "staking a claim" means taking irrefutable ownership of anything, material or nonmaterial, it originally meant to drive a stake into your land claim to demonstrate to others that it belonged to you. In addition to pounding in a stake with the homesteader's name attached in the center of the claim, some would mark a piece of land as "taken" by digging a hole, showing that a well had been started, or by driving four posts into the ground, representing the beginnings of a house.[26]

If the land was government land, the claim was filed at the nearest government land office by payment of a small fee and filling out an application stating citizenship or the intention of becoming a U.S. citizen. However, just because a settler selected a location for his or her farm, there was no guarantee he would get it. Someone else may have already filed on it, and claim jumping—the stealing of another's claim—frequently occurred. In Oklahoma, where much of the state was settled by land "runs" into territories opened at a specific date and time, legal battles ensued over "sooners"—those accused of entering the territory and selecting their land too soon.

Although the majority of settlers arrived on the Great Plains almost penniless, they frequently felt exhilarated. Having successfully completed a long and difficult journey, many believed they had untold opportunities before them. They were excited to be landowners, and that, combined with the exotic vastness of the prairie, caused many to comment that they had never felt better or healthier in their lives.

IN THE LATE 1850s, many people who were settling eastern Kansas favored it becoming a free state or a slavery state. The author of the letter below, a so-called "free-stater," settled in Osawatomie, Kansas—a hotbed of the antislavery movement.

At the time, the community had such notable residents as John Brown and his sons, who later led the slave rebellion at Harpers Ferry. People in the eastern United States longed for information about the characteristics of the Great Plains and the opportunities that existed there, which the author, Jane Carruth, enthusiastically obliged. Like many settlers, Carruth and her family arrived before the majority of their possessions, and they were forced to make do—living in a tent with a makeshift bed, borrowing everyday items, and finding creative uses for the few objects they had. She sent this letter to a distant cousin, and her letters were also published in a newspaper in Watertown, New York—the community she had lived in prior to moving west.

Osawatomie, K.T. [1856]

Dear Cousin Melinda:

I have kept my promise so well in writing to you that I need make no apology; it is enough to say that I have little to occupy me in this land of promise. I wish that you and many more could see with your own eyes; you would almost think that you were in the same garden that our Mother Eve was in. James was afraid it would be too level for him, but in that he is disappointed—such beautiful swells of land; I cannot convey its beauty to your mind.

We arrived here safe and pretty sound, considering all things, and are quite happy in our tent on the ground. The land surveyors have been around to-day, and it don't give us quite the spot that we expected; but it is all good, only we love to get the best. The heavy timbered claims are all taken about the country, but good chances for buying out those occur often.

We have corn growing in the field, and peas and bean and potatoes in the garden. Things don't mope here; they jump. We have not heard about our things yet, but think they must be in Kansas City by this time; but we don't have mail but once a week, so that we don't get the news in a minute. What things we have were lent to us.

You may ask "What have you to use?" In the first place, we have two sheets that I had in my trunk that Mrs. Dorn washed so late that they did not get packed with the rest; those we have basted together and filled with prairie-grass; that, crosswise, makes a bed for all our family; under it we have brush, to prevent dampness; everything being put out of doors every day and our tent raised from the ground to air it perfectly. Some young men of our company who had trunks of bedding lent us some, so that we have a very good bed and sleep very sound

Now, for eating. Our old bread chest is our table; I had two bowls and some cups in one trunk, and our old knives and some spoons, and at Kansas City our company bought some tin plates, so that we have three of those;

those, together with some pail covers, when we have company, make our dinner dishes; for stove I have all outdoors; for oven I have a spider [pan with a lid and three legs] a little larger than ours, belonging to one of our company. In this I have had some good shortcakes and fried cakes and pancakes; once I went a mile and baked some raised bread at a neighbors. I have one iron kettle that will hold a pailful, and a teakettle that was lent me by a Mrs. Brown from New York City; the kettle had been used to whitewash in, and then left out of doors; and I can assure you that it has had many a cleaning to get it fit for use. This I use to heat water, wash dishes and boil clothes in, and then have to clean it to make hasty pudding in.

Most of my work has to be done outdoors and at a great disadvantage My arms have been blistered from my elbows to my hands. James has had his back blistered once. We all look as though we belonged to the South. In earnest Albert's face peels off every few days, his skin is so tender. Walter runs into all the mischief he can find. Having no table to work on makes my work very handy for him to "help." He is almost the color of the Spanish Santa Fe traders that pass through Kansas City.

July 5.

We received letters from Mr. and Mrs. Snyder, also papers the 1st day of July. They were very welcome.

Mrs. S. wants to hear all the little particulars; so that, if you will, you may let her read this. She'll want to know what we have to eat. We have a cow that gives four or five quarts a day; will be a new milch cow this fall. We have bread, hasty pudding (my favorite dish, also the childrens), butter, tea, coffee, goose-berries (the wild, very nice). I had some dried fruit with me, I have some fried cakes. This is about the substance of our fare. If we always have as good we shall not get very lean. Yesterday, July 4th, I had calls from five ladies at one time, some of them from town; some of them have hard times here. They have passed two winters here—the first delightful; the last, like ours in the north, severe. We have had very hot weather all the time since we arrived in the territory. The thermometer stands, at eleven, at 104 in the shade, but I like it. We don't have, or have not yet had, any of those sudden changes. The country and climate are very delightful.

On our claim you can see twenty miles or more. We have land that is 100 feet above the river; it is so charming that I wish, and often, too, that I could lend Mr. Snyder my eyes and have him here a little while. When viewing it, my mind involuntarily reverts to Doctor Watt's, "All on those wide, extended plains shines one eternal day."

How I wish that thousands of our poor but worthy people could be transferred here; what homes they could have, instead of spending a poor existence where they never can rise above poverty. It is dear living here at present, but as soon as people can raise things it will be cheap.

A settler's possessions being loaded into a Great Northern boxcar for the journey west

July 11.

I don't know when I began this, or when it will get to you. It has made some difference about my diligence in writing, feeling that you might not get it. It is said that the "border ruffians" have to see the inside of the free-state people's letters Here we have no law except what people carry in their own hearts. When a pro-slavery man wants to take a claim from a free-state man, he gets some of the lawless ruffians to go and drive him off by threatening death in so many minutes. One not far from us was so treated in the night this week. I hope that their reign is almost over. If the people of the North could only see how little real principle there is in slave power, they would never kneel or bow down to it any more, but, let civil war or disunion or what not come, stand for right until the cure of our nation is driven into the gulf below it.

I write this with baby in lap, holding book on my knee. I hope that you will enjoy the reading as much as I do the writing. I often wish that I could monopolize a telegraph I would often converse with my dear friends in Watertown; but with children in my lap and at my elbows, I find little time for correspondence. Lucy has been sick for two weeks; is getting better. Most of our Jefferson county boys have been sick; they have worked too hard.

I don't know what to say about your coming here, I think you would do well here. They have no milliner here; but how well you would get through I don't know. It is said that two companies from Indiana have been robbed and sent back to Alton. One of the Grants has gone back, and when the other is going we don't know, but not soon. If you could get in one of those companies that we came in, you would get along well enough.

I must stop for James is going to town, and I want you should get a letter from Kansas. There are good chances to buy out good timber claims from those who want to leave. I think it will be hard to drive the free-state people from Kansas; they came to stay, and they calculated to do so.

If Mr. Ingalls [publisher of the *New York Reformer*] wants anything from my letter for his paper, let him have it; if you are willing he should read it I thought it might be a little amusing to Watertown folks to see how we live.

Write soon Write all the news
Jane Carruth[27]

COMPETITION FOR THE BEST LAND *in a given region on the Great Plains was fierce, with some settlers even ignoring marks of ownership, like a stake in the ground with a name attached. Thus it became common for settlers or homesteaders, once they found a claim, to race to the government land office to file it. It was not unheard of for several parties to attempt to file on the same claim on the same day, sometimes within hours of each other. Once the paper was filed, claimants had six months within which to begin making improvements to the land or risk losing it. The undeveloped nature of the region, transportation difficulties, and even weather—as was the case for this Civil War veteran—often meant delays that could be fatal to ownership of a piece of land. Disputes became widespread, occasionally causing outbreaks of violence, and they often had to be settled by the courts. Those who lost the court battle were forced to start the process again, in many cases moving farther west in search of new claims. The author of this letter is asking the Iowa adjutant general—who oversaw that state's Civil War regiments—to intervene in the dispute over the ownership of his claim.*[28]

Horton, March 3 1874
Mr Baker
Dear Sir

    I thought i would write you a few lines in regard to my homestead. i being a solgier i came out here Sept the (17) 1872 and located my land and went back to Ill to git redey to come out here in the next Spring 1873, the winter being cold bad that i could not git here til late, the roads being bad and the water being high so i did not git here til june the nineteenth day. i came from vermillion Co Ill, it being 675 miles when i got here i found that a man contested it and he was a living on my land. i being a solgier i think i had aut to have my homested reward. The goverment has got my money and land. i sent pappers to washinton last Sept sign and sworn to by two witniss stating the caws why i could not git here sonner and they was singed at the land office at Sioux City and i have not herd from it yet. i thought you being state official and the state of iowa oes it to me i being one of her solgiers. i belong to the 20th Iowa infantry Co E. I am a poor man; want a home that what i came here for. i [thought] you mite have some influnce on the land office at washinton. Let me here from you soune.

    yours treuly
    J. W. Fuller
    Direct to Bigelow
    Noble Co Minn
    i live in Osceola Co Iowa[29]

THE PLATTE RIVER VALLEY on the northern Great Plains served as an artery for people traveling into and through the region. It included such famous routes as the Mormon, Oregon, and Pony Express trails and later became part of the roadway for the nation's first transcontinental railroad. The trails cut through the treaty-owned land of several Indian tribes, including the Lakota and Cheyenne. Violence eventually erupted between Indians and settlers, and detachments of the U.S. military were sent there to forcibly restore peace. Traveling from Baltimore to Denver in 1866, a year after the attacks reached their height, Edward Nicholson recorded his journey along the Platte River in his journal, noting the trail of grave markers along the way. Two years later, in 1868, the Lakota signed the Fort Laramie Treaty, under which the United States agreed to establish the Great Sioux Reservation in what is today western South Dakota and to respect the tribe's unceded lands in eastern Montana and Wyoming. After gold was discovered a few years later in the Black Hills of South Dakota, the U.S. government broke the treaty, and the tribes were eventually forced onto the small reservations where they reside today.

While tales of conflicts between American Indians and settlers have become part of the folklore of the Great Plains and the West, in reality far more pioneers on the Platte River trails died from disease, accidents, and drowning than from Indian attacks.[30]

June 1st, 1866

Quit camp at 5.45 A.M. Morning clear and sun shining with great heat. Traveled 12 miles & encamped. Broke camp at 1 P.M. At 2:15 sky cloudy and a storm seen in the distance. Drove 14 miles this afternoon which time a rain came upon us and we encamped at 5.15 P.M. ⅛ mile east of Fremont Springs. At 6.30 sky still cloudy and threatening rain. Two of our party, while walking behind the wagon this afternoon, came upon a rattlesnake that they succeeded in killing without much difficulty. Along the rout I noticed the graves of 4 men: 3 of whom were massacred by the Indians last Autumn, the other, about 2 yrs. ago.

[June] 2nd. Broke camp at 6 A.M. Opposite Fremont Springs are the graves of 5 individuals, four of whom were supposed to have been killed by Aborigines. East of "O'Fallon's Bluff" is a grave, the head board of which bears the following inscription: "Wm. Viougt shot Sept 15th, 1865. Age 31 yrs." I am told by a reliable gentleman that he was shot by a cattle herder. Very possible for a trifling breach of freighters rules. How many poor mortals have lost their lives while crossing these plains, by the inhumanity of individuals, calling themselves men!

Crossing O'Fallons Bluff is a beautiful route, rather wild and romantic. The Bluff is the terminus of the line extending for hundred of miles east of the river or rather the western terminus of the eastern extension of the Bluffs. The Bluff is named after a man who has a ranche near by. It stops abrubtly and slopes almost perpendicular to the edge of the River. Further along the road is another grave, bearing date 1864. Saw several antelopes and one prairie wolf [coyote] during forenoon travel. Saw 10 or 12 graves east of Alkali Stn., three of the first Nebraska Vet. Cav.[alry], killed by Indians Oct. 22nd, 1865. One of the sixteenth Kansas Vol. Cav.[alry]—died in Spring of 65; the other graves were marked by plain boards only; bearing no inscription. Had some rain during afternoon. Encamped west of Alkali Station at 5.05 P.M. Sun set clear and beautiful. A strange country this; rain and sunshine every thirty minutes.

Sunday, June 3d. Had stewed wild duck and gravy for breakfast. Quite a treat for this part of the globe. Morning fair and pleasant. Resumed our travel at 6.40 A.M. and encamped for dinner about ¾ miles from the South Fork of the Platte. Saw a great deal of Cacti and prickly-pear along the route today. Encamped for the night near the river.

[June] 6th. Last night was very cold, like wise this morning. Started our journey at 5.45 A.M. Traveled through a portion of the "Great American Desert" and found the sand very deep. The bluffs are very beautiful in appearance—sand in some places formed like riffled snow drifts. The wind blew from the west early in the morning, but shifted around to the south at about 9 O'Clock. Left noon encampment at 1:45 P.M.—road not quite so sandy. Wind blows from South and very hard. Encamped for the night behind the ruins of what was formerly a dwelling etc destroyed by the Indians. The wind continues and has raised to a small hurricane at about sun-set, and a fearful storm is seen rising in the West. This ominous appearance in the elements but deepens the gloom of the picture before us. The dwelling of a fellow mortal leveled with the ground and pieces of stove and cog wheels scattered around open the way for deep reflection. The appearance this evening was awfully grand and wild, eclipsing any storm or violent action in Nature that I have ever saw. This place is called "Lillion Springs" (there being a spring just in front of the ruins). On the hill opposite, may be seen four graves: One of which bears the inscription on the head-board A.C. Lewis, another Kate Haunter, Canton, Ill., Age 2 yrs, 3 mos. 4 days, another Geo. Smith, age 26 yrs. Killed by Indians July 29th, 1865; another bearing only the following—killed by the Indians.

[June] 7th. Morning clear but the wind still high, having shifted from the South to the West and afterward to the North, when we had it both

A tent was often the first residence when families made a claim on the Great Plains, 1886.

strong and cold. After traveling eight miles we came to a stage station; on the hill opposite are three graves marked as follows—C.A. Lane, aged 21 yrs. Killed by Indians Oct. 29th 1865—Killed by Indians; F.A. Buckston, 3rd Cavalry, aged 26 yrs. Killed by a comrade, July 14, 1865. After traveling a few miles we came to a ranche, opposite to which, on the hill are two or three graves—one marked E.C. Freeman, killed by Indians, Oct. 21st, 1865. Two boards broken down and writing effaced. Encamped at 11.30 A.M. and resumed our journey at 1.20 P.M. Crossed a sandy ridge and came to Moore's Valley ranche, where are four or five graves containing the remains of individuals murdered by the Indians. After traveling a short distance I saw a grave on the ridge, near the road Inscription: R. R. Bailey—killed by Indians June 12th, 1865.[31]

THE EXPANSION OF RAILROADS in the late nineteenth and early twentieth centuries enabled settlers to make the journey to the Great Plains via train, find their land, and then return later by train—accompanied by their possessions. When they returned, they often brought wagons, horses, and even building materials, with which they could construct rough claim shacks rather than the sod houses more common in the previous decades. In a 1905 letter to her sister, Georgia "George" Townsend describes her journey with family members to establish her homestead. The party took the train to western North Dakota and then transferred to wagons for the remainder of the trip. The twenty-six-year-old Wisconsinite—who viewed homesteading as an adventure as much as an economic pursuit—led the procession part of the way on her bicycle.

After living on her homestead claim from 1905 to 1908, Georgia made proof—fulfilling the requirements of the Homestead Act. She returned to Wisconsin, spending the rest of her life there as a single woman and teaching school for many years. Data from North Dakota show that women were as likely as men to fulfill the requirements of the various land acts.[32]

Gladstone, N.D.
April 28, 1905.
Dear Joan:

I have arrived. Don't misunderstand me. I don't mean in the French sense of the word but simply that after many and diverse stages I am on the S.W. quarter of Section 6, Township 145, Range 94, with a rice pudding boiling on the "parlor cook[stove]."

In Madison I piloted Aunt Mollie around and she had a real nice time, we added some stuff to our lunch as the things looked so tempting. She got potato chips and I got pickles and radishes and it was all mighty good. Our train was just pulling out as the Northwestern was pulling in so of course I didn't get my watch. At Tomah about fifteen people got on the train who were all coming out here [to settle] and Mr. John Bailey got on some place up there and went as far as La Crosse just to visit with papa.

When we reached St. Paul the men had to go to the depot to see about our tickets. As the baggage was very heavy I proposed that Aunt Mollie and I stay down on the N[orthern] P[acific] platform and save that long haul. We stood there watching all the other western freaks when who should dash up but Billie Overson with a box of flowers and a big box of candy for me. Flowers seemed a bit queer considering the trip but they have been just lovely; a week today and they are still fresh although they have been in a box most of the time.

Between St. Paul and Minn[eapolis] we were delayed about two hours by some freight cars off the track so we never reached Gladstone until 5:00 P.M. Wednesday and the boys got in about 10 P.M. that same night. Gladstone isn't much of a berg and a pitcher full of carnations and jonquils was quite the making of the hotel. The beds were clean and the eats very good.

Thursday we unloaded all day and early Friday morning Ringling and his circus left the town. I led on my bicycle; Cass followed with his horse Boxer and my democrat wagon [flatbed wagon with bench seat] loaded with necessary leftovers. "Bill" with a load of lumber and the portable house came next and then Harland on the band wagon with the other democrat wagon as trailer and another load of lumber and then Ringling himself in the top buggy with Aunt M[ollie] at his side and the fool pony for his steed. Uncle Ed rode wherever he could drape himself for the time being.

The parade moved on majestically for about twelve miles when coming down a little hill dad touched the pony with a lath (his septer and whip) and its heels flew in all directions but most particularly at the top buggy. Father whacked and Aunt M shrieked: "Catch him!" Of course Uncle Ed and Cass ran to rescue their wife and mother by each grabbing an end of the beast. He calmed down again until about noon when the order of the parade changed and Ringling and his white charger led and I came next. The rest of the men were away behind. Then the pony let loose again and papa jumped for his head and Aunt M got out as best she could. Then there was a waltz on the prairie but dad waltzed down the pony and he was ugly. Harland came up and we got him unhitched and tied to a post then ate our lunch and wondered [what to do]. When Uncle Ed caught up he proposed blindfolding him so Aunt M got on a load of lumber and father and Uncle Ed drove the pony. His temper continued rather ragged but he kept his heels down.

We travelled twenty-eight miles that day and stopped over night at a Mr. Watkin's place on the Knife River. He is an old Englishman and talks like a story book and has white hair that stands all over his head about three inches. Mrs. Norton can't touch him for funny expressions. His wife was visiting at one of the neighbors, so one of the riders and I started supper. I can't say that things seemed very clean but they were very pleasant and we soon forgot it.

The ranch belongs to a big company and the real manager was out on the range but his organ was there and of course I must play. You will know I was discomfuddled [about performing] but finally he got out a hymn book. But I did my duty like a little man and pumped the organ and sang to beat the band, while he bellowed bass in my ear. It was great; we had lots of fun.

The next morning we left early and soon I was in country I knew, so I rode on ahead and called on all of my old friends. I got into Connolly's for a late dinner, very hot and rather leg-weary but glad to have arrived. After dinner they hitched up and we drove out and rounded up the straggling circus parade and all pitched camp on my land as it was Saturday night and they thought it would be too hard to start and run two camps. I gave Mrs. Connolly some candy and sent the flowers home with her. Cass went over on the water wagon [and] she sent back a pail of milk and five or six dozen eggs for Easter. The tents were up, supper was ready, the portable house went up by lantern light with just a few whacks Sunday morning. The flagpole also went up Sun. morning and I raised the flag.

All but Harland and I went to hunt Uncle Ed's land and get a little coal so we had dinner at night, hams, eggs and so fourth. Our callers numbered thirteen on Sunday and three yesterday. This morning Uncle Ed and Cass started for Gladstone again to get the rest of our things and, as we brought only the bare necessities, we have eaten off of pail covers and tin plates with my brass hairpin tray for a sauce dish and only owing to an oversight in my packing we have a spider and a little bit of a kettle to boil potatoes for seven. Hellick Tostenson being with us is building my house, which is progressing famously. Papa and Uncle Ed have the bed, Aunt Mollie the cot and the rest of us the ground, which is very comfortable.

Sunday night they all gathered in our tent and Aunt M made me read the Easter service and besides we both wore our new Easter (sun) bonnets. Last night they wanted more reading so I looked up the Battle of Waterloo and read to them by candle light. Of course father snored.

Dirty! You never saw such a dirty bunch but there is very little wind and the mornings and evenings are beautiful. The meadow larks sing beautifully and altogether it is fine and dandy. The coal bothers a little yet as it is damp but the Connollys dumped a lot of oak posts in our wagon when we went for water yesterday so we get along alright. I seem to be chief cook and

I told Mother I didn't like to be my own trumpeter but I didn't believe that Father need be ashamed that I was only a girl.

I think if I write any more you will never be able to flounder through such a waste-of-time thing. I hope you are feeling better and are having nice sunshine like we are. Irma had a nice long letter waiting for me at C[onnolly]'s.

Love to all

George [Georgia Townsend]

P.S. Forgot to say my nose is peeling.[33]

A LARGE NUMBER OF SINGLE MEN from the United States and abroad, the majority of them working class in origin, came to the Great Plains in search of free land. Believing the promotions of the regional boosters and railroads—that, given seeds and plow, the land would bloom with unrivaled agricultural products—the men saw the taking of a land claim as a means of achieving prosperity.

Young men from other social classes also felt the lure of free land, including this young letter writer from England. After living briefly in Jackson, Michigan, he wrote his father in England asking for a loan to help establish a farm in Kansas. Originally a member of a homestead "colony"—a group organized to help homesteaders settle in clusters on the prairie—he viewed a farm as the way to generate the means to return to England and bring his betrothed back to the United States with him. His ambition, fueled with the claims of Great Plains promoters, made him overly optimistic about the crop and livestock potential of the region.

Abilene, Kansas

March 5, 1871

Dear Father & Mother

I am a long way from Jackson just now. I have long explanations to make before you will understand my position. About Feb 16 a young man that was intimately acquainted with Elijah and Rufus Judd and me came to Jackson & told us that a colony was formed for going into Kansas to locate & settle a new town in a southern county. We had a good talk over the advantages and disadvantages of the chance & came to the conclusion that it would be a good chance to make a living easily & honestly. So we got what little money we had at command & started on the 24 day of February. It cost us 26 dollars to come from Jackson to Abilene. These men or several of them started about a week before us & said they would wait on the road

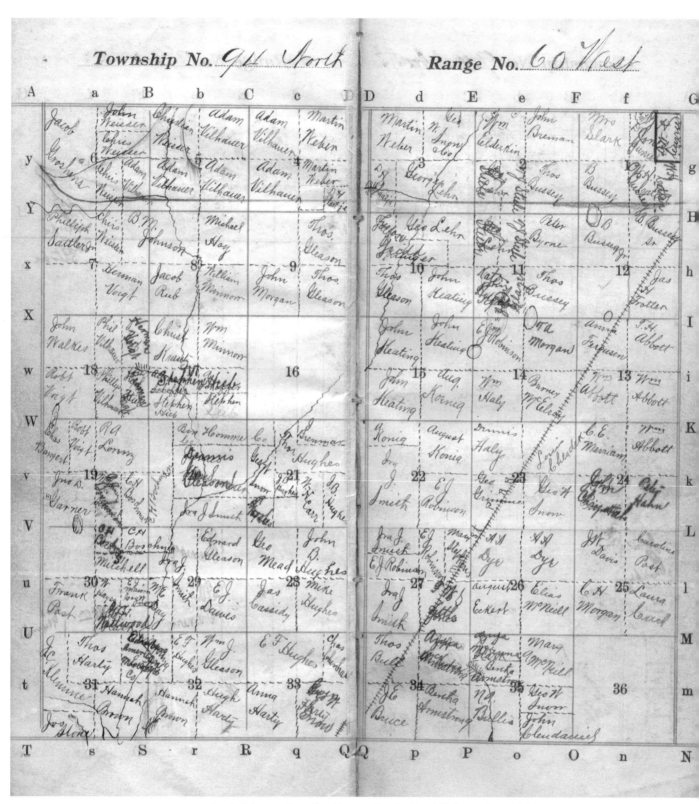

Land claim map from Bon Homme County, South Dakota, about 1891

till we caught them & all go on together. But when they got nearly there they found that the trustees they had sent out to locate our lands, instead of studying our interests, had located lands for themselves without regard to the colony & therefore every man had got to shift for himself.

We have been round the country & I never saw so fine a country in my life. This country is all government land & free for all. By taking out my naturalization papers which would cost me a dollar I can go & pick out 160 acres of as good land as I ever saw anywhere in the state, provided some other person has not made prior claim. That 160 would only cost me 14 dollars payable at the end of the year. I should have to reside on that land 6 months out of 12 every year for 5 years, then I should send to Washington & receive my deed of the farm from government, & if I choose to before that time was out I could sell my claim & improvements. That is what is called a homestead. This same land can be bought from government for 1¼ dollars per acre payable in a year. Emigration to Kansas is greater now than it ever has been known to before, for many farmers from the eastern states are coming here & when they see the country they sell out [and] buy here of government or homestead 160 acres.

The climate here is splendid. When we came through Chicago & when we left Jackson there was a foot of snow on the ground but there is none here. The weather is splendid. This is the best cattle raising state in the union & last year this state took the premium for fruit. The country is not settled much but in two years I think it will be far in advance of many of the old states. Cattle will live and thrive on grass all winter here & in Michigan we have to stallfeed them six months. The farmers grow 25 bushels of wheat to the acre here with just ploughing about 3 inches deep & I am satisfied by ploughing 8 or ten, I could raise 45 to 50. Two horses like yours would plough 8 inches deep without any extraordinary effort. I should be all right for horses for I could buy Texas ponies off the herdsmen very cheap & they are much hardier than native horses. Cattle are shipped on the cars from here every year by the thousand & last year the number shipped was 200,000 heads, two hundred thousand cows & bullocks. They are driven from Texas; that is 800 miles & often one gets lame or too poor to walk & they can be bought very cheap from the herdsmen. Then the herdsmen have to ride their horses so much that they often get tired or too poor, & a very little money or a "good watch" will buy them. So if I see a good chance to trade my watch for a Texas horse I believe I should not be doing wrong to trade it. I do not want to part with it but it was given to me to benefit me and I do not know how else it could be of as much service to me.

Wheat costs nothing more than the cutting & thrashing when a man gets well started. There is enough timber here & plenty of water & some grand prairie. Tobacco grows well here and cotton would do well but nobody goes into that class of farming at present. The weather will be hot but being on the prairie the wind will keep it from being hurtful. Trees grow well here where the fires have not destroyed them. The Indians have been in the habit until lately of setting fire to the prairies so that they could be [traversed] across and I believe that is what has kept the prairies from being covered with timber. I have conceit enough in me to think that with a little help my fortune is made. I mean by a fortune that I shall not ask any odds of anybody any more than one man would of his neighbour. I shall have a good occupation, honourable, healthy, constant and there will be nobodys will to serve, save my own.

Dear father this is a great chance to make money if I had enough to buy me a plough & wagon & harness & provision, enough to last till I get my crop. I am about to make a very large request I hope you will not think it too large. If you could spare me 80 or 100 pounds I could have a farm that would be worth 6 times that much in 3 years. I should be able to send you a great part of it in 4 years if necessary. I have been making calculations on good & bad & with the amount of expences that I should have to pay & I see no drawback at all. There are plenty of men that came here 2 & three years ago with but little means more than a pair of horses & wagon that are worth 3 and 4 thousand dollars and the chances are just as good as they ever were or better for they have stood out the hardest of times and made a market for produce of all kinds. Mr. Henry (the man whose office I am writing this in) thinks you had better send a London draft on some New York bank by a registered letter to me. I am going to work for Mr. Henry tomorrow for 2 dollars a day. He has got enough trees to plant out 20 acres of orchard with trees of all kinds so I am likely to have employment that will suit me. I can buy if I have the money this summer perhaps 20 Texas cattle for 10 dollars a piece & next year they will be worth 20 & a year later they will be worth 30 & are not any expence more than fencing which would have to be done anyway. Any amount of people have made their start in "doing well" by buying those cattle & a horse and herding them on the prairie for awhile till they get fat and that costs them nothing.

Dear father I have given you a truthful account of the state of Kansas as far as I am acquainted with it & I shall be able in time to come to give you more. I believe I have found the place that suits me exactly. I should have written sooner but your letters have not been sent on to me so I do not know what they contain. I am very sorry to hear of Mrs. Goughs almost sudden death. My poor Lizzie must feel the loss of her Grandma very much. Keep her spirits up. If you can. I believe the day is not very distant when I shall have made money enough on my farm to have a trip and fetch her. I feel confident I can do it if I have a start. I hope you will write to me soon so that I can tell what to be doing. Here the soil is as good and as deep as our garden and all it wants is a man that is not afraid of ploughing too deep and that is me. Dear father & mother I should like very much to see you and my chances for doing so are better now than they ever were before. I do not know of any thing more to write of this time so I must conclude with

Best love to all I remain

Your affectionate son

Thos Butcher

PS Please direct to me at Abilene Dickinson Co Kan[34]

The attractiveness of free and cheap land to people of limited means meant that many settlers and homesteaders arrived almost penniless after using their limited resources to pay for the journey. Their financial condition became acute when they were met by drought or grasshopper outbreaks that made it very difficult to earn a small income from farming, to find a job, or to produce food. The author of this 1873 letter and her family made the two-hundred-mile journey across Minnesota in a wagon to their new farm. When they arrived in Marshall, they lacked the money to pay freight charges on their clothes, furniture, and farm equipment, which had been shipped separately by train.

In her letter to her aunt who lived on the East Coast, Mary Carpenter describes their difficult circumstances, as well as her lack of enthusiasm over the primitive turn her life had taken. Her aunt responded by sending five dollars to help with the freight costs.

Marshall, Minn, July 10, 1873

Dear Aunt Martha

Your long and very acceptable letter came to hand last Monday. I had one from Mother the same day, also one from Mrs. Walker an intimate friend in our old home. Excuse my using pencil, as our ink is packed with goods we have not got yet. This paper is dirty and wrinkled but it is all I have at present, and no means to get more with. You kindly said that everything about our affairs would interest you so I'll try to tell you just how we are situated. Please ask Cousin Laura to take this letter as if written to her also for I may not be able to get writing materials and stamps to write again soon.

We arrived a week ago last Monday after a journey of two weeks. George and the children drove the stock on foot while I drove the load. George did not ride ten miles of the whole distance 200 miles. The older children took turns riding and driving. We camped in our wagon and cooked our meals by camp fire. I was not romantic enough to enjoy it much, but endured it better than I feared. My health and appetite were very poor when I started. They have improved. I can work better than when I started.

Our circumstances now are very discouraging. George is haggard and worn for his mind is ill at ease and he works very hard. The freight on our goods was nearly 90 dollars. Thirty of it is yet due, and we have no means of raising it. The goods are at the depot only four miles off and have been for several weeks but we can't get them. I am afraid they will be sold to pay freight. Most of our clothing, etc. is there. The bureau and large wooden cupboard and several barrels crowded full of clothing, household stuff, etc. All my baby clothes are in the bureau. We have a horse we expected to sell, but find there is no sale for horses. There is no chance to earn anything in this region. The grasshoppers have destroyed the gardens here so all we have is a few potatoes growing. We have everything to buy till we can raise something excepting our meat and potatoes for awhile and not a bit of money. Our appetites are good which seems rather unfortunate. No house but a leaky ten foot shanty. We expected to build something right off— mother said when we started "you are going there to freeze and starve next winter." I thought not, but George said today it might prove so.

We have sacrificed considerably just to get here. It makes it worse that I expect a confinement [childbirth] in October. My health is pretty good now, and if we had a decent house, and our goods here, it would look much brighter. George has learned to make brooms and if he could get a little money for stock he might do pretty well at that during the winter. Lumber is ten miles off and we have all the wood to buy before we haul it. I try to trust in God's promises, but we can't expect him to work miracles now-adays. Nevertheless, all that is expected of us is to do the best we can & that we shall certainly endeavor to do. Even if we do freeze & starve in the way of duty, it will not be a dishonorable death. I laid awake almost all night, one night, worrying about it but that didn't do any good. "Suffering to the day is the end thereof." We have a little to eat yet and perhaps some way will be provided for more when it is gone. We sold all of our cows but two and a young heifer. Our best cow was sick on the road and does not yet recover. She will be no dependence this winter. The other will give milk in a few days, but we shan't have much butter to sell. The first two years will be hard very probably. If we struggle through them, then we stand a chance to do pretty well I think. As to clothing will have to do almost without I guess. We came very poorly provided for in that respect—By the way, when you send mother's box, if you happen to have any old things that you don't think worth mending they would do us lots of good. I am an adept in using old things up, having served a good apprenticeship. Mother will forward to me.

We are not able to subscribe for any papers. It is lonely enough without reading. We left our books with Mother for fear they would be spoiled before we got a house—perhaps you have some old papers to spare. They would be appreciated. Do you not think me a consummate beggar? I'll run the risk of you thinking so—I am afraid you will not want to hear from me very often if I have nothing more cheery to write. Perhaps sometime it will be better. Our cookstove stands out of doors with no protection. Isn't this roughing it? You hope a double portion of the pioneering spirit descends to me. I am endowed with my little of it. My taste runs the other way to conveniences, elegancies, comforts and all the paraphernalia of civilized life.

The country here is very pleasant in Summer. We have the [railroad] cars in sight for several miles here. The children are well and hearty and all send love to Aunt Martha. We had a good celebration of the "Fourth" at Marshall. Good speaking, singing, etc. Mamie and I went down with Mr. Ross' folks our nearest neighbors. I took our team last Sabbath and Mamie and I went to meeting at Marshall. Congregational preaching in the forenoon, then Sunday School and Methodist preaching in the afternoon. Both sermons were good and the S. School interesting. My shoes were too poor to go and I had no gloves which did not correspond with the rest of my dress, but I put aside scruples and went. Geo. has no pants fit to wear, so he can't go. I have a number of things to fix over for the children but can't do it because we can't get the goods. If I had fifteen dollars we could get all except George's machinery, reapers, horse rake, plough, etc. That fifteen dollars don't grow on every bush. Well, I mustn't worry. I should not have troubled you with all this only I could not tell you truthfully how we were situated without. Don't worry about it. I presume it is all for the best. "It is always darkest just before day."

Mother's health is better than when I came away. She wrote that Father and Frank were feeling quite debilitated by the hot weather. Willie was well. Father thought he never should see me again when I started off. All the hindrance will be lack of means. It takes ten dollars to go there but a day and a half on the [railroad] cars will take me there. I am owing Mother a letter, but am dreading to write for fear it will worry her. Tell Cousin Laura I am always very glad to hear from her and will try to be prompt in replying. Please give my love to her and Cousin Lorell and say I have not forgotten the pleasant times we used to have in Fall River together. I cannot form much idea of your Connecticut home as I never was there. I don't know of any news to write. Do you want to know what our carpet is? Our cabin has a ground floor and we spread green grass over it for a carpet and change it occasionally. It saves sweeping and mopping. But I would rather have a chance to do both. We brought a dozen hens with us, so we have some eggs. Our pigs could not travel so we had to sell them all except two which we brought in the pork barrel. I am not fond of salt pork but it is a good deal better than no meat. George desires to be remembered—he feels better to be on his own place than he did where we were before. If we can get through next winter I hope we can do pretty well.

With love from the children and myself to all and hoping to hear from you before long.

Your affectionate Niece,

Mary E. L. Carpenter[35]

A SETTLEMENT PATTERN quickly emerged on the Great Plains. The first arrivals established farms. This wave included land speculators who were there to make the minimum improvements on a piece of land and then sell it or exchange it for a mortgage. After the first settlers, towns sprang up on the prairie. They usually held a post office and the offices and homes of land locators, farm merchants, bankers, hotel operators, and others who catered to the business of agriculture and the influx of people. As the number of farms grew, additional settlers, including this young attorney from New York writing to his mother about the uniqueness of the prairie and his prospects for success, arrived to set up service-based businesses. Churches and schools came along quickly.

Railroads were crucial to a town's future. Many towns, including the one from which this letter was mailed, had their prosperity cut short when track surveyors bypassed them. By 1900, Swan Lake had ceased to exist. Ironically, today when areas on the Great Plains lose population, the process reverses itself. As the number of farmers and ranchers declines, communities begin to lose service industries and boards start to appear over the windows and doors of main-street businesses. The final coffin nail for a town on the Great Plains was, and is, the loss of the school and post office.[36]

Swan Lake, Dakota Territory, June 17, 1878

My dear Mother

No doubt by this time you are all wondering where Ed is and what he is doing. I have serious thoughts of pitching my tent right here for a time at any rate. This is a village—not as large of itself as Topurtch but probably a hundred times the amount of business done here. It is the county seat of Turner County—situated on the open prairie. Not a fence to be seen in any direction—the air is so clear and light you can see farm houses nearly 10 miles away—perfectly level. The country is being settled rapidly with a very industrious class of people who of course have taken up Government Lands under the preemption laws. They are termed "claims." A great many Russians of the class called "Minonites" are locating here about. I am the only Lawyer in the county and I think if I can induce one other to come I can at least make a good living from the start and in 2 or 3 years some money.

The nearest place to this is 30 miles distant by stage but 30 miles is not far. We take an Indian pony and canter across the plains very easily. We expect a railroad here in a few months. I find I am only about 185 miles from Tim. About 50 miles across the prairie and then take the cars. If I succeed here I will make a visit in time.

I wish you could see this country and the immense fields of grain on the Prairie. There is one whole quarter section about a mile distant (160 acres) of wheat nearly ripe. It looks grand. I tell you, this country air makes me feel like a different man. We have an Episcopal church here—a great many Baptists too who hold services in the School House. Of course I will have

Hart and Company putting down a well on the semiarid Nebraska prairie

to take a leading part in churches & everything for a Lawyer in a place like this is expected to do the talking for the whole town. Of course I expect poor picking for a time but am confident if I stick to it and am deserving of it I will meet with fair success. The People here seem very anxious for me to settle with them and hold out every inducement to me. At any rate I shall stay here until I find by experience it is a failure. It rained every day from the time I left Chicago until I arrived in Swan Lake, when it stopped. We have no wood in this country except as the settlers have planted—Prairie Grass is the fuel and Sod the building material with straw or hay roofs until they make money enough to buy wood 50 miles distant to build houses. Our feed is not of the best but if a fellow is not too sensitive on the taste, he will get along by keeping one eye closed & feeling his way through the hash.

Well I will close—have so much to say I spoil it all in trying to say anything. I will try and write regularly every week. Let me know when you receive this—tell Jennie and Harvey to write often and you & Father write when you feel like it.—a letter from either of you is a treasure—

You will probably learn by piece meal all about this new country as I write from time to time—and let you know how I prosper &c.

With much Love to you all

I am your affectionate Son

Edward C. Kennedy

Turner Co

D.T.

Swan Lake is so named for one of the prettiest lakes I ever set eyes on being situated here—The Indians called it "Owl Lake."[37]

SOME OF THE MOST DRAMATIC SETTLEMENT EVENTS on the Great Plains were associated with the opening of tracts of land in what was known as Indian Territory, later the State of Oklahoma. In 1887, the U.S. Congress approved the Dawes General Allotment Act, which converted tribally held lands to individual ownership under the belief that it would assist American Indians in becoming self-sufficient landowners and farmers. While tribal members were given specified tracts of land, the remaining so-called surplus lands were opened to non-Indian settlement. This policy fragmented reservations throughout the Great Plains. The Dawes Act is viewed by many as one of the most devastating blows to the nation's tribes and their land holdings, for it had the effect of reducing tribal-owned land by 87 million acres before it was repealed in the 1930s. In Oklahoma, lands that had once been set aside for In-

dians (including the "Five Civilized Tribes" forcibly moved there from the southeastern United States on the infamous "Trail of Tears") were initially exempted from the act. Then in 1893 the federal government began negotiations with these tribes to extend Dawes Act provisions to them, with the remaining acres parceled off and made available to non-Indian settlers through runs and lotteries.

Land runs were just that—a mass of humans, animals, wagons, and trains charging into newly opened lands at a set date and time. The runs took place in Oklahoma in 1889 and several times in the 1890s. The author of the long letter below, a Kansas attorney, participated in the 1893 run for the purpose of claiming a lot in the newly platted town of Enid, Oklahoma. To his sister he describes the chaos associated with the event, as well as the fact that his brother had been falsely accused of being a "sooner"—someone who searched his or her land prior to the predetermined starting time. While "sooner" was originally a derogatory term, Oklahoma is now known as the Sooner State.[38]

Wichita, Kansas
September 19, 1893
Dear Sister:

This finds me, so far, on my way home from the opening of the famous "Strip." As I have several hours yet to wait, I shall attempt to give you an idea of what I have seen. The "Cherokee Strip" as you know is a large body of land about 120 miles long by 90 wide, a part of the Indian Territory, and joins Kansas immediately on the South. About 1840, this large body of land was by Congress set apart for the Indians to pass over in going west to hunt. Such a strip was called for because of the great slaughter the tribes would inflict on each other when they would attempt to cross disputed territory for any purpose. But all of this is a matter of history, and now to my trip.

I left home a week ago last Monday, had passes to Oklahoma City. Got there without event and took the "Chawkta" road over to El Reno. Visited at Franks one day and then took the Rock Island to Hennessey where Guy lives, and which point was one of the principal starting places for the great crowd when the signal was given at 12:00 o'clock noon on September 16th. Hennessey had 15,000 people when it ordinarily has only about 700, so you can judge of the jam. I say you can judge of it, but no one who was not on the ground can get the faintest conception of the situation.

Guy, as Postmaster, had made extensive preparations for the jam, but it had exceeded all expectations, and as soon as I got on the ground I was installed as money clerk, stamp seller, and deliverer of all mail beginning with the letter B. In this capacity, at an over crowded window, I worked steadily for two and one-half days, and by the way, it was most awfully tiresome work. Besides myself, there was brother Don, who got there some days ahead of me, Guy and two very active and experienced lady clerks, and among us we managed to keep the letter mail straight. The paper mail [newspapers?] was given up, and then thrown into a hopeless mass in one corner of the room, no effort being made to do more than take care of the letters.

Settlers camping with portable stoves on the westward trail

The line of the strip is about four miles north of Hennessey and along this line for days, the anxious throng had gathered and were gathering. Government troops paced the line and held the surging crowd at bay pending the signal, which was to be the firing of a cannon at 12:00 o'clock noon on the 16th, as before stated, when a free-for-all race was to be indulged in with "The devil for the hind man," as was said so often by the "Boomers" along this line. Great suffering prevailed. Instead of remaining at a suitable place, where water and food for man and beast could be had, the excited and anxious crowd hugged the border to the "Promised Land," and of the 170,000 estimated to be anxious for the race, large numbers perished from the lack of water mostly, and also on account of lack of food, and the excessive heat. Twenty-five innocent children died in one afternoon at Orlando, and this alarming death rate was almost, if not quite, equalled all along the line. At Hennessey, a woman passed me with a little child, limp and pale at her breast. She was crying but the little one was beyond tears. I asked her what was the matter, and she said, "Oh, sir, my poor baby is dying for water and I have no money with which to buy." I quickly got the water and as it was put to the little one's lips, it drank, but a look into its little face told the tale too well. I saw the mother the next day but she was alone and the look of despair on her face told the story. This is only one of the many cases. Water sold for five cents a drink, and those that did not have the five cents went without. Many old people and those sick or disabled found graves instead of homes in the New Country. I think while I was there, I spent $5.00 for water. I don't want to leave the impression that water is hard to get, as it is in far western Kansas and eastern Colorado when they dig over 300 feet for it, for this is not true. The wells are shallow and the water good, but this surging mass of humanity never thought of wells or of water. A little concerted effort would have supplied the entire throng with plenty of good water.

For fear I have left the impression that there were large numbers of women and children in the company, let me also say that there were but few as compared with the great number of men; but the Lord knows there were far too many.

There were two ways of going in, one by railroad, and the other, a "free-for-all-go-as-you-please."

Guy and I had in view the town of Enid, located by the Government, 17 miles from the line, directly north of Hennessey, and conceded to be the best town in the Strip. The way to go was bothering us. The train was limited to 15 miles an hour, and whether a horse could be found that would make the race quicker than the train was the question. A man offered us a Clay Bank "cow horse," for $60.00 upon these terms: one of us to ride him in, and if he got a good business lot (the race was for lots as well as farms), we were to pay him $60.00 for the horse, whether we killed him or injured him in the race, for his use. If he did not get us there in time, we were to pay only $5.00 for his use, whether we killed or injured him, or not. He was a strong built, tough-looking horse, and we concluded to take the offer, and Guy to ride in for "blood," on the Clay Bank, and I to go in on train, and we to share our fortunes, which ever way proved the best. We were bound to win either way, if I was hustler enough to hold my own with the 13,000 estimated to be in the 46 cattle cars composing our train, and drawn by three engines. Well, by great effort, I got on a front car up on top where I could jump off easy and run from the train to the desired valuable lot. At last the cannon shot greeted the ears of the wild "rabble" and "Ye Gods," never in the history of the world was such a wild charge made. The greatest army that ever moved in a charge was not composed of any such numbers, and this is true of all the world's history.

Thousands of horses were run down the first mile and exhausted, fell back dead losers, while old farmers in their lumber wagons made "claim-getting races." Race horses dropped dead in their tracks, killed by fool riders. Up until I was twenty years old, I was almost raised in the saddle and I know the capacity of a horse. This is also true, in measure, of Guy. We talked it over with care and agreed that whatever the crowd should do, Guy was to keep out of that awful dust even if he went a mile out of the way, and also ride slow to start with, even if the crowd left him miles behind.

When the wild rush was made, nothing could be seen from the moving train on account of the awful clouds of dust. The train was crowding and passing thousands in a very short distance. When out a few miles, I stood up on my seat on the top of the box car and anxiously gazed into the clouds of dust behind for the Clay Bank, but in vain. Then presently, far in the rear, I could see a Clay Horse passing nearly everyone. As mile after mile passed by, the noble horse came faster and faster, and at 12 miles Guy was side by side with the train and the vast crowd was some miles behind and others scattering along between, while only a couple of dozen were ahead, and some of them a mile ahead. But about this time the train had to make a stop and the Clay Bank then had the best of the race and it was settled that the horsemen would beat the train in.

Guy's whip was at his side and he leaned away forward and held his position in the saddle as perfect as a jock of years of experience. It was now a race of horse against horse, and not of horse against train. I could see from my standing point my brother catch up with a crowd of about sixteen to eighteen running in a bunch. As he approached them they sprinted for a half mile, leaving Guy a little ways behind but he did not urge the Clay Bank at all, and soon he was among them again. One fellow made another sprint and drew away a little but the rest were content to keep along side of Guy. Soon, however, the fellow ahead sank back to the crowd, and then, for the first time, Guy called on the Clay for more speed, and said to the fellows, "I am going to quit you."

It was the first time in that awful race that he had called on the noble brute for a higher rate of speed, and he was asking him to go faster in order to leave behind, horses that boasted of generations of running blood in their veins. As he urged him, the Clay Bank quickened and lengthened his stride. The other horses, responding to the whip, stayed with him only a short time and then Guy was running alone. There were seven still ahead of him, and his first idea was to overtake them, but better judgement prevailed, I think, and he lowered his rate to where it was before he drew away from the seventeen, and though gaining rapidly, he went on to the townsite of Enid, the 8th in the race, close on the heels of the seven blooded race horses ahead of him.

The train had to pass the town before stopping, but I did not wait for a stop. I climbed down the outside of the cattle car, watched for a smooth place to light, let go and lit with a terrific jolt, but "right side up with care." Recovered from my shock, I ran for dear life and found Guy holding one of the best lots in Enid for himself and also bluffing the people there off one he was holding for me and the bluff worked—for I got the lot without any-one claiming against me.

Guy and I grasped hands, he standing on his lot and I on mine. He only pointed at the panting Clay Bank and we stood there, our eyes filled with tears, "The heart must speak when the lips are dumb."

But now the wild crowd from road and train are upon us. I could not begin to go further. The Clay Bank was eating in twenty minutes from the time he landed on the townsite. He was rubbed down and received the attention Nancy Hanks gets, or better. It is needless to say the man got his $60.00. Guy wanted to pay the full amount and keep the horse. I had no use for him and was glad to let Guy have him. He declares the noble brute shall live and die his undivided property.

Brother Guy got a contest on his lot. A man claims it because he thinks Guy a "sooner," that is to say, he thinks he started before the signal because such a horse as the Clay Bank could not have made the race with the horses he came in with, and in the time he did—fifty-seven minutes. But he is fated. We can prove just when he left by dozens that knew him, and saw him start at the signal. But true to my luck, I had no contestant at all, ex-cept a little squint-eyed mean looking, sneaking cuss that got on the rear end of my lot and claimed me to be a "sooner" too. He was there for blood money and I ran a great "sandy" on him. Learning his claim, I said, "My friend, I came in on the train and if I am a "sooner" all those on the train were "sooners." If you had anything like a legal right, I would respect your claim and let the courts settle it, but as it is, I don't propose to spend any of my good money on you and you get off right now or I will kick you off in short order." He hesitated only a moment, and he was gone, and he was the only man that ever molested me.

At noon yesterday (Monday), I sold my naked interest in the lot for $300.00 spot cash. But as I owed all my success to Guy, I arranged the matter by letting him have half the money and he lets me have half the interest in his lot. Before I left, we rented his lot for $45.00 a month. We two put up a building, the renter furnishing all the money but $50.00 and taking it out in rent.

I shall go back and try the contest case. George Willis is here, he made the sale and we gave him 5% or 15.00. Then too, Brother Don made the race and got a good farm, but has a contest which I must fight for him. He is "dead broke," and Brother Guy and I staked him to the tune of $35.00 out of this money. So $50.00 went for lumber, $15.00 for commission and $35.00 for "staking" Don, leaving just $200.00. I took a $100.00 bill and gave Guy one. So I am that much ahead if I never get another copper.

There is a rival town two miles away which promises to make the Government town a hard fight and should it win, my lot would be worthless, as would also Guy's. We thought best, therefore, to let mine go and keep his, another such move as my going on the train and he on horse back, a sort of sure play which ever way it goes.

There were many funny, and many sad things that came under my notice; a consumptive rode a race horse in and got a good lot, but was so overcome that he almost died when he half got off and half fell off his horse. We got liquor and water and braced him up a little; put a shade over him and had him resting quite easy, when a man about the size of Libby came up and said, "What is that _____ doing on my lot," and taking the poor devil by the leg, began dragging him face down, through the almost unequaled dust. I think I am not putting it too strong when I say that 50 men went after that big fellow, smashing him in the face or any place they could hit or kick him, and he got away. Such another mortal was surely never seen. He was not badly hurt, that is, not seriously hurt, though he could not stand up when I left. He thought he could impose on a sick man, but he got left. We gathered up the consumptive, washed his face, put another drink in him, got him back under a shade on his lot and there he stayed and up to the time I left, there had not appeared a mortal man who dared claim his lot.

I walked from one town to the other Monday, and to avoid the dust, which is simply beyond endurance, and I think must be the ruin of this country, I walked out in the grass a quarter of a mile from the road. As I came to a swale grown up with salt grass eight inches high, located in a [prairie] dog town, I said to myself, "Here is where rattle snakes should be if there are any in this country." Just then, that awful, frightful, rattling hiss sounded by my feet. I always dreaded a rattler and as this one was the first

I had encountered for years, I think I jumped ten feet the first time and was out of the swale in an instant. Once on short grass when I was safe, I stopped and was gathering myself together, and trying to compose myself, when a tall, stern fellow, wearing glasses and riding an Indian pony, came in the direction I was in and halloed out, "What's the matter? Have you got the jim-jams?" If there is anything on earth an Indian pony fears, it is a rattle snake. I have ridden those ponies a great deal and I know their habits. They are a race to themselves. Indian also fear those snakes more than the whites. This lean, lank, duck was on a regular Indian pony with the slit in its ears and every other mark of his breed and to reach me, he had to cross the swale. I said to myself, "You'll have the jim-jams, if that snake has not crawled away." And sure enough, just as he got to where I jumped, the pony whistled and lunged, the fellow threw both arms around the pony's neck and did not quite go off. The pony, once safe out of the swale, at once stopped and the fellow gathered himself together and rode over to me and said, "Say, what was that?" I told him and he said, "I never saw one alive, lets go and find it." I said that I hadn't lost any snake and if he wanted to hunt rattle snakes in dog days in grass such as that, to go ahead, but I would not join him. He wouldn't go alone, but tried to ride the pony back into the swale. The pony had more sense than he did and would not go a step beyond the short grass on the edge of the swale.

Jennie, the dust down in that country is beyond description. Here, we have sand. The dust here is not fine. A piece of sand gets in your eye, you fish it out, cuss the country a little, and life is tolerated in the windiest weather. But down there, the dust is as fine as the finest bolted flour. So fine that the gravitation of the earth has no attraction for it and some of the time the sun was darkened with it. Every face was as dark as dirt could make them. It killed me almost. My throat is in bad condition and I could not live there at all. The dust will be the ruin of the country. El Reno is bad. I don't think I could live there, but it is pleasant compared with Enid. I slept in a tent, caught cold, and was in bad shape, sore and stiff and worn out, and was longing for "Home and the dear ones far away." In fact, in that condition, and covered with dirt from head to foot, I caught a north bound train on the Rock Island. The train was so full that I had to ride in the water closet.

When we got to Pond Creek, in the Strip, who should try to get on but Bi Hutchins. They refused to let him on, telling him he must wait for the next train. I knew his voice, raised the window and asked him to ride in my apartment which was strictly private, but which I always shared with my closest friends. He accepted the invitation and with the assistance of the fellow with me in the closet, pulled him up the side of the car and through the window. He rode to Wichita in the closet.

I got off at two o'clock this morning, at Wellington, went to the hotel almost dead and the dirtiest man on earth, I think. I washed for an hour, getting off the rough, then went to bed. Got up this morning and spent about $5.00 for clean underclothes, white shirt, stockings, collar and etc. together with shaving, shampooing, and bath. Feeling better after this, I started for home, reaching here a little before noon. I came near throwing my dirty clothes away but took them along, knowing that Etta would call me extravagant and extremely foolish, etc. but if she ever cleans them I shall be fooled.

George Willis is in partnership with a fellow down there and they are making $8.00 or $10.00 a day making filings. This will last several days.

Horse-drawn wagons loaded with supplies on the Colorado plains

George was feeling good but oh, how dirty. I could write much more, but I began this letter at 12:30 and it is now just 4:00 o'clock.

Should the Lord, in doing all things well, call me hence very soon, or permit me in his wise providence, to see many years and a ripe old age, the memory of my trip and the opening of the Cherokee Strip will never grow dim, and will ever be a green spot in the history of my life to which I can look back and see "Hope and Despondence, Pleasure and Pain, mingled together, Like Sunshine and Rain."

Give my love to all and write often.

Lovingly,

Brother Preston[39]

John and Margret Bakken (with young daughter and son) stand by their expansive frontier sod home. This photo inspired the Homestead Act centennial postage stamp.

Homes of Sod and Tar Paper

After the Great Plains settlers claimed or bought a piece of land, they wasted little time before beginning to build their homes and outbuildings. They did this not just for the shelter. If they were filing for land under the Preemption or Homestead Act, a house was a requirement showing that the claimed land was being "improved." As the house was being constructed, the homesteaders lived temporarily in tents, in their travel wagons, or, if they were lucky, with a neighbor or friend whose house was already built.[40]

Homesteaders commonly built houses out of logs if their claims were near rivers or streams or the mountainous western border of the plains. Out on the open prairie, settlers built homes of earth—the most readily available building material—by stacking up alternating strips of thick prairie sod. People also lived in dugouts, which were cut into the side of a hill or into the ground and given a sod or thatched roof. To increase the earthen homes' comfort and appearance, they often plastered and covered inside walls with wallpaper or cloth.[41]

Later, when the construction of railroads facilitated the transportation of building materials, the claim shack became a more typical home. Aptly named, it was little more than a tar paper and board shack sitting on the land claim. Shacks were ice cold in the winter and smelled of hot, melting tar in the summer. As more and more settlers staked out claims in a region, they also built schools and churches, often of the same materials as houses—logs, sod, and tar paper.[42]

The physical evidence of the ingenuity and resourcefulness of early settlers and homesteaders can be seen in the surviving remnants of their homes and buildings. Sod houses still dot the Great Plains, although most are museum displays and preservation sites because of their fragile condition. Claim shacks also continue to survive. A primitive forerunner of the modern prefabricated house, they provided inexpensive and simple housing on the treeless prairie. While many lie crumbling, most ended up as additions to farm and ranch houses or as tool and equipment sheds. The unique architectural styles of individual groups of immigrants, including the Scandinavians, Germans, Dutch, and Finns, are also evident in many of the early barns and churches that are still in use throughout the region.

IN THIS EARLY LETTER from the plains, writer Phebe Clark proudly provides her uncle and aunt in Indiana with a written tour of her new log home in eastern Nebraska. People who settled an area first, such as Phebe and her husband, who worked in real estate, chose sites near rivers and streams, if they existed. Unlike most of the Great Plains, those locations often provided a supply of trees for lumber, fences, and firewood, as well as a second benefit: a dependable source of surface water. Fort Calhoun, Nebraska, named for John C. Calhoun, the South Carolina statesman and orator, sat adjacent to one of the sites where Lewis and Clark had camped during their journey up the Missouri River.

Fort Calhoun [Nebraska] Sept. 18th, 1856

My Dear Uncle and Aunt,

Well, Uncle Van, the time has come, the good time we used to talk about, when we settled in our own home and I am "Monarch of all I survey, of my right there is none to dispute" where I have a right (my husband willing) to say to an intruder "Puck-a-chee," and as I never knew what it was to be so situated before, I do enjoy it supremely.

You have heard of me often through others, I could have written to you before but you know I told you I was going to wait until I "got good and ready" that means until I got our house arranged as I wanted it then I promised to let you know.

Ft. Calhoun is our stopping place, it is situated on a beautiful Plateau on the Missouri River sixteen miles from Omaha the capital and is the county seat of Washington County. In the town there is a hotel, grocery store, blacksmith shop, courthouse, a mill and a few dwellings. There is plenty of timber close to the place, and several good springs of water, there is a good landing place for boats, though none have stopped yet.

E. H. Clark and Co's cabin is situated on his claim (which joins the town on the north side) just at the foot of a bluff, which is as high as Bald Hill, that celebrated place to which all you folks resort for pleasure rides. Thank fortune we don't have to go so far to see a hill. It is not as sloping as Bald Hill and we intend to plant a grove of forest trees all the way to the top next spring. The main travelled road passes a few rods from the front door, there is room between the road and the field for a block to be fenced in which is commenced to be done now, which we intend to ornament and give the dignified title of "The Park" and it is possible that when the fence is nearly completed a deer or two may be caught napping and on waking will find itself fast, though I think it more probable that said deer-park may be dedicated as a calf-pen first. True it would be quite a coming down, but the usefull comes before the ornamental you know. We have a garden enclosed, two locust trees of good size before the door, they are higher than the house. But now [we] will just take a peep within doors and see what a good housekeeper Phebe makes. I don't allow any comments to be made, you must take things as they come, making all the necessary allowances for new beginners.

I'll give you a seat in my rocking chair whilst you take a survey and a very comfortable one you'll find it, hair bottom, cane back, and cherry frame. Well the house is a hewed log house twelve by twelve in the inside, will be

A log cabin, the preferred home for families fortunate enough to settle near rivers and streams, with adjoining addition made of lumber

chinked and daubed. At a first glance you would think the walls were lathed and plastered but look a little closer and it is only lined with white muslin. The walls we intent to paper over the muslin this winter leaving the ceiling white. A good ingrain carpet covers the rough boards, but they are not rough now for I scrubbed them smooth before the carpet went down. The front door faces the east and the Missouri; we have a view of the river from two points. As you come in just turn to the right and look at yourself in the looking glass and do not be astonished if your face has turned a shade or two darker since you left Laporte for this is a great place for people to tan. If you were here you would be in the top of the fashion for everyone is dark complected. If they aren't when they first come they soon get so.

Next look out the window and take a view of our glorious cornfield, "Old Muddy" [Missouri River], etc, a chair is on each side of the window, next comes Fan's chair which is in the corner, turn to the right and next is a table, and a nice damask tablespread covers it, then a chair, then a lounge covered with striped green and white furniture calico it has a pillow which makes a very good place to rest onesself upon. Then you turn corner, the second a chair, then a door opening into the kitchen, then another chair and you come to the grand stairway which makes the third corner, then a chair and the remainder of the south side of the house is filled with books, Hick's law books most of them, a bookcase reaching from the ceiling to the floor will not hold them so the remainder we piled up behind the door which makes corner the fourth and thats all. We had a clock but it was not worthy a place as it would not go, so we helped it down and laid it on the shelf and a watch is in its place.

You must not slight the kitchen for there is where the good things to eat come from. There I will not be so precise in describing fearing to tire you. Suffice it to say it is a little place twelve feet by eleven, contains a bed for our old scotchman, some of Hick's own handy work, a table, cupboard, stove, and all the appurtenances thereof, a water bench, flour barrel and a trap door to get into the cellar, a couple of chairs, and several utensils without which the kitchen furniture is incomplete. It is a little place to have so much in, but when everything is in its place there is plenty of room for a little body like me to turn around in. I have a nice cool cellar with shelves all around it which stand certain ominous looking jars, covered up tight but which are found to contain preserves of different kinds, as strawberries, tomatoes, plums, and which are a very good substitute for citron, some tumblers with grape jellie.

Now for upstairs and if you are not a lazy man you will want to mount the steps, no matter if they are not so easy of ascension as your own. I'll warrant them to be as good as your cellar steps. Now I suppose some would call my upstairs a garret but it is my bedroom and I sleep just as sweetly in it as though it were a palace, the walls of it are lined with white muslin also. I have two beds in it, one of them another specimen of Hick's work, both of them have mosquito-bars around them and they have been a source of comfort to us this summer, two windows on the east and west, oil curtains to them, four trunks and a box to hold bedclothes in. We have straw matting on the floor though we have enough left of the ingrain to nearly cover it this winter and a couple of chairs and that is about all. We have to make our wardrobes on the walls, and you must be tired so come down and lay on the lounge and rest.

Well I have given you a complete description of our little domicil and it may seem silly to you, but remember it is written at your own request. Now perhaps Camille and others of the girls think, well I don't see how Phebe can be willing to live in such a heathenish country. WHY! My Good Gracious! Girls, we are not at all out of the world. People think, act, talk, walk, and halloo "Hurrah for Buchanan" just as they do in the states exactly and I know if you all had as good husbands and loved them as dearly as I love mine, you would be happy in any place with them. Here I imagine Uncle Van says, "Oh the honey-moon with them is not over yet." Well I hope it never may be, they say "contentment is happiness," if so then I am supremely so, as indeed I am. We have two horses and a buggy, a lumber wagon and yoke of cattle, a cow and calf, a pig, sixteen chickens, a cat and dog, and a BABY.

I make all our own butter and you just find better sweeter butter than it is if you can. I wish I could send you my last churning for to taste and I can make good bread and we have every good to eat that you have except sweet potatoes and apples.

I have one good neighbor. The rest place us (very kind in them) among the aristocracy so we don't have much to do with each other. There are a great many fine families living in Omaha that I think much of. I wish they were nearer. Now Uncle and Aunt I try to just [do] the best I can keeping house, and I succeed pretty well I think. I am perfectly contented and if you can say as much no doubt you are a happy man. I am afraid my guitar is lost; we have never heard from the box that Father sent us.

We have most excellent health here, have not been sick a day since I came. No disintary or diarrhea in the county, not a case, so it's the very place for Aunt and Father. All the sickness seems to be chills and we have escaped them so far. Fan lives on melons, green corn, cucumbers and anything she wants and has never had the slightest touch of diarrhea. She is the pet of Ft. Calhoun, and is happy as a bird. Now you must not think from what I have written that I am glad to be away from you all, no I often think of you and some time I'll be there to see you. We are blessed in one particular where you are not, that is we have no flies of any consequence. Hicks says it is because we are cleanly.

You did promise to answer this Uncle Van and you must remember it very soon,

Give our love to all

As Ever

Phebe A. Clark

Since writing the foregoing Hicks and I have had a few of the nicest little chills in the world but I guess we drove them out with quinine. And I have just had a tooth drawn which has been aching more or less ever since I have been here.[43]

Sod houses were an ingenious answer to housing on the tree-less Great Plains. While their design was simple, construction was anything but easy. Homesteader Uriah Oblinger describes the process to his wife, whom he missed dearly, while he, like many other men, located and established his claim prior to having his family join him.

Because of the value of sod as a building material, Oblinger stripped his sod from the adjacent property owned by the railroad rather than use his own. Vast quantities of land had been given to the railroads by the government as an incentive to lay track, and the resentment this created may have fueled his decision to use the railroad's sod. The railroad land grants were the beginning of a long and often tumultuous relationship between Great Plains agricultural producers and railroads.

Bachelors Hall, Neb, Fillmore County

April 6th 1873

Dear Wife & Baby

Giles & Sam have just finished each of them a letter and have gone in the other room to visit the folks in the east end of the house and here I am now at the table hurrying my pen over the paper talking to those I love through its silent medium. I commenced my sod mansion last Monday and took some of the material on the ground such as brush & poles. Tuesday it misted rain some so I could not work at it, Wednesday I broke sod & commenced laying the walls, hauling the sod about 80 rods off of R.R. land. Why dont you get it on your own, you ask? Well we are not going to use our own soil to build with when the R.R. owns every other section around here. I am building my walls 2½ ft thick and have got them 3½ ft high, but the weather today and tonight looks as though I would not do much at it tomorrow. This morning when we got up it was misting rain and this afternoon it snowed some and tonight (for I am writing by candle light) the wind is blowing from the north and looks as though it would freeze some befor morning. Well if it will give us a good rain it would do us good for it is dry here so that the dust blows my eyes full and makes my face all dirty. Now I expect you think being so dry the sod would all break to pieces. Not a bit of it. You can grab a piece 10 ft long and start off with it and wear it out dragging and not tear it. I cut my sod 2½ ft long and plowed about 4½ in' deep & 10 in' wide and it is pretty heavy work to handle them. Oh! yes, while I think of it, the first meals victuals I ever eat on my claim was last wednesday at noon. It consisted of six cold corn cakes with apple butter spread on them. There was to be preaching here today and the weather was so bad that no one came. It was to bad was'nt it for Giles made a general cleaning out yesterday and when I came in last night he would hardly let me put my feet on the floor. I suppose you would like to know the size of my house (I wont say ours till you get here). It is 14 by 16 ft inside, is this room enough for you to spread out in, if it is not I will build larger this fall and take the present one for a stable.

Ma I got no letter yesterday and I wanted one so bad for I felt a little

African American homesteaders in Oklahoma outside their sod house and dugout (at right)

anxious about my little Pet since she is going to have the measles. If the weather is such tomorrow that I cannot work at my house I will go to the P.O. and ask the P. M. about it and mail this one also. I am in hopes this is almost the last letter I will have to write for I want you and baby to answer in person pretty soon. If you get to come at the time appointed it will only be two more sundays till we will be together if delayed a week it will be three, but dont risk starting with Ella till it is perfectly safe. Now Ma just fasten your head on good, for the wind will blow it off if you dont. Sundowns [hat with wide brim] like you used to wear would be good in this country for they would develop the body running after them. And fix your eyes to quit looking at fences for we have none here. only little pig pens and very few of them yet. We had a little sing just now. Tell Nett I am get to be quite a soprano, have almost a female voice, at least I would like a voice of female just now. I have realized this winter more than ever before that it is not good for man to be alone.

You say I have had two men with me, well thats true but 20 men cannot fill the place of one woman. But I suppose you think just to the contrary, well we wont quarrel about that till we get in quarreling distance. I am getting a little tired of S[l]apjacks for once. I begin to want some bread that tastes like if a womans fingers had been in it. When I went to the Blue [River] after wood I would get Mrs Dewolf to bake me some biscuit and it tasted awful good, I tell you, but then it would taste better seasoned with Matties fingers and then her & Baby to pour my coffee & help eat it. You see I am writing this part of my letter in a whisper for fear some one will hear me. Dont tell Nett or she'll laugh at me and that will make me feel ashamed. Ma I had to get a right hand plow because they had no left hand ones to sell, it goes very awkward for me. I tell you I wont use it any longer than I have to. Ma if all goes well you will get to see Jenny when we start from Crete to my homestead (not ours till you get here) for I will be there hauling off my corn right where she is. I expect she has her baby by this time. Now Ma dont get mad for saying mine not ours for you know every body in this country is called a bachelor till he gets a woman to live with him whether he is married or not. Some try to make me believe I am not married. They tell me they dont believe I have a wife for if had I would have her with me. They tell me they dont believe if I had a woman I could stand it away from her so long, they are only joking you know.

I have lots to tell you when you get here so just make up your mind to listen and dont bring any deaf ears out here with you but enough of this nonsense. I am enjoying excellent health at present and hope you and Baby and all the friends are doing the same thing. No more for tonight but remain your affectionate Husband & baby's happy Father

Uriah W Oblinger[44]

Sod houses were so prevalent during the early non-Indian settlement of the Great Plains that in some regions they were often the only style of structure visible within a day's journey across the prairie. Even barns and fences were made of sod. The uniqueness and primitive nature of the sod dwelling, coupled with the simple lifestyle of most farmers, caused many settlers, like the author of this letter, to explain their living arrangements before friends or family visited. Some were even hesitant to tell others that they lived in a sod house.[45]

May the 23rd, 1886
Dear Mag

Your and your husband's letters was gladly received last night. We were glad to hear that David & Fred intend coming out the 1st of June. Hope that they will not be disappointed. I wish that you & Sarah were coming too. I think you might if you made some exertion. We shall look for you.

Now in order that you will not be disappointed in regard to our mansion "as to what it is made of" I shall give you a few remarks. It is neither

A prairie family wearing Sunday-best clothes gathers at a frame house boasting a shingled roof and insulated with blocks of sod.

made of brick or stone, the outside being chiefly made of sod and instead of plastering it is ornamented with tar paper on the inside. Just fancy how beautiful it must look. And instead of rooms partitioned off, we simply make rooms which we can take down to suit our convenience simply made of calico. Or if it isn't necessary we have no rooms at all. Well I guess I won't inform you or the men folks the other conveniences we have for fear we might not see them. We had rather wait and tell them the rest when they come. At any rate I shall venture to say that if they write the day that they will be in Northville so as Dave can meet them I shall have a grand supper prepared. The bill of fare consists of buffalo beans, bran bread & water. Now I mention this part of the fare so as they may not expect anything better. I do hope they may come & enjoy themselves. I only wish that

Civil War veteran Sylvester Rawding and his family outside their sod home with glass windows in Custer County, Nebraska, 1886

you could or will come too. If you can't I should be pleased to see some of the children. Tell Fred the same. I received Ada's picture, answered Phebe's letter, have been to service & prayer meeting today, got dinner & now I don't feel any too smart to write. It has been a very hot day. We just had a little shower. We need rain very much.

Well I must draw to a close. The children are bothering me, so with love to all I remain as ever,

Yours Truly

Mrs. Sarah E. Williams

Roanoke, Faulk Co.

D.T.[46]

LIFE IN A WOODEN CLAIM SHACK on the prairie was often a rough existence, as described by this settler. He and his brothers—veterans of the Confederate army from Alabama— moved to Colorado to make their fortune in farming and to cure their respiratory ailments. Many early Great Plains homes were poorly built and sparsely furnished, so much so in this case that the author tried to dissuade his father from sending their sister to stay with them.

After living in Colorado for six years, the lifestyle, combined with their lack of success in farming, caused the brothers to return to Alabama.

Arapahoe Co, Colorado Territory, Wednesday July 22 1874

Dear Father

Bro Johnie rec'd your letter of July 14th yesterday. I will proceed to answer your questions as accurately as possible. There are three rooms in our house, two of them are 16 sixteen feet square each. The other which we use for a dining room and kitchen is ten by fourteen. Our house was built with green lumber, consequently it leaks very much whenever it rains. Besides Galpin is a miserable poor carpenter & all the work about the house is awfully botched up. I don't believe that we will be able to live in it ourselves this winter like it is now, much less Sister Laura, besides I don't think it would pay to have it fixed up. It would be best to build a new house entirely. It certainly couldn't be plastered, the rain would beat the plastering down the first time we had one. The house is put up so badly & the timbers about it are so light that it will take it its best to survive the winds of the coming winter. I hardly think it will be safe to live in this coming winter & I know I wouldn't live in it the next. It would require a good deal of work to make it comfortable.

As for furniture we don't keep the article on hand, but then we have a substitute, Viz. two large pine boxes 7½ feet long by 4½ feet wide, with four legs attached to each. The depth of these is about one foot. One of the boxes is filled with hay & covered over with bed ticking on which Bro F sleeps. The other box is filled up with an old spring mattress, the wires of which poke up about six inches mashing a fellows ribs flat with his back bone which sometimes not infrequently causes him to have unpleasant thoughts in his dreams. On this last described box & mattress Bro J & my-self sleep. These two articles constitute what is in Colorado called beds. We have three bags, three feet long & one & a half wide each, made of old bed ticking that I think must have come out of Noah's ark. One of these bags is filled with wheat straw which was harvested probably the first crop after the flood. The other two bags are filled with wool, but as for the color of the sheep from which it was taken, its hard to tell. Judging from its looks the sheep couldnt have been black or white either. We will say six of one & half a dozen of the other. That would bring it up to about dirt color. These three articles we call pillows minus casings. We have five pair of blankets (all red) which cost $5.00 dollars per pair, very common blan-kets of course. Six wooden bottom chairs two water buckets, made of pine, one dipper (tin), one looking glass & comb & brush, one lamp & two chim-neys (obliged to keep one extra one on hand), one rough pine table about 3½ by three & a half feet square (this we use for all purposes, to eat on, write on etc.), seven plates, one dish, one bowl, one pitcher, seven pewter tea spoons, one pewter table spoon, & one big iron spoon, six cups & seven saucers (Bro F broke the other cup), six case knifes (three varieties) five forks (two kinds), one tin pan which we use for a sugar dish, one large tin pan for washing dishing in, one tin pan for making up bread in, two coffee pots, one good size one & one very small one, the largest one we use for cooking coffee in, the other we use for a molasses pitcher (whenever we have any). I forgot to mention, when I told you we had two buckets, that we also have a wash pan, we have two shelves nailed up in the kitchen to put dishes on. Havnt any safe [cupboard] of any kind to put them in (or the surplus food we frequently have on hand). Now for the cooking uten-sils, Viz. one kettle, one spider, one bread pan (hardly large enough), one tin boiler, one iron pot (hold about 1½ gallons of water), one cooking stove, one coal scuttle & two shovels, & last of all a coffee mill. I don't think I have left out a single article that's worth mentioning & whats here is pretty much as I have described it to be.

As for our ability to meet our liabilitys, it will be impossible for us to do it. I don't think we can even make running expenses. The grass hoppers are eating up our wheat & what few vegetables we have, besides the sale for vegetables isnt near so good as we thought it would be. About getting those notes renewed, the terms etc, I can't say much about them, I am in-clined to think we can do it however, but Im afraid on no better terms.

Money is scarce out here & commands a big interest. As I have said before, refined society in this country is very scarce & I don't know who Sister Laura could associate with, on terms of equality. She is certainly far superior to any one I have seen out here, both in refinement, intellect & everything else you can think of. Of course there are some pretty clever neighbors around us with pretty good sense, but that's about the best I can say for them. It would take a good deal of money to fix things comfortable. You see we havnt any conveniences at all. Such as bureaus wardrobes, wash stand, towels, beds, & bed clothing, etc. In fact there are a great many things that we haven't got, which we ought to have if sister Laura comes. Every thing taken in consideration, the want of society, the scarcity of money & above all your not being here yourself, I hardly think Sister Laura ought to come. Of course we would all be perfectly delighted to have her here, but circumstances are such that I really dont think she ought to come yet awhile.

I think it would be advisable to let Bro Hines come on as soon as possible. Im afraid that Bro Johnie has injured his lungs very much by having to cook. I heard him say yesterday that he believed he was worse off than when he left Alabama. He has been spitting blood for the last ten days. I think I am better off than when I left Alabama. Bro Frank is decidedly better off. I think the sooner you send Bro Hines out the better, then the climate will be more effectual in curing him. I dont think I shall go up in the mountains as I half way expected to do when I wrote you last. I think a trip up there would help me a great deal though. I wrote you on the 9th & 19th of this month. Bro John is now writing you. Had a good rain yesterday evening. Our wheat looks pretty well but the grass hoppers are eating it up. The neighbors wheat will not be hurt by the grasshoppers, as it is about ready for harvesting.

Love to all & write soon to Yours etc.

Joseph E. Hall[47]

In this letter a newlywed describes the "queer" living arrangements of the western South Dakota home to which her husband brought her—"900 miles from nowhere." Sod houses and dugouts were an efficient home on the prairie, and claim shacks were inexpensive and easy to put up. After a few good crops, however, settlers who intended to stay, like this couple, replaced the dwellings with frame houses. Wooden homes afforded more comfort and room, and they signified financial success and increasing social status.

This letter, sent to Lottie Chesnut of Woodstock, Illinois, was discovered in the 1970s when a homeowner found it in a wall

while remodeling. He gave it to his local historical society,
which donated it to the South Dakota Historical Society.

2-21-[19]08
Dear Lottie:

 After all I'm not so worse considering the time you left me waiting am I? And writing this too when I ought to be getting dinner. There's no surprise now in me telling you that a married woman writes this, is there? But perhaps it's a surprise to tell you I haven't forgotten those nice door curtains you made me for a wedding present. [I had] double doors made in my new house just a purpose for them. So don't put off making them like you put off answering letters, will you.

 I must tell you about my new house which I wish you could peep into right now. First, I'll begin with getting married. I married the farmer boy I told you about. I left Anaconda [Montana] the 4th day of December and visited at Sioux Falls and Dell Rapids. Quit at my school + taught last winter. Then I went to Parker, and we were married the 19th at the

The Odegard homestead's frame house and outhouse in North Dakota, built with lumber probably carried to a siding by railroad, 1901

Methodist ministers as there was no Cong[regational] Minister there. We surprised everybody as we had told no one we were going to be married. We drove out that evening to Frank's brother, and then Lizzies, my best friend, and maybe they weren't greatly surprised. They wouldn't believe it until we showed proofs. We stayed with them until Monday, and maybe we didn't catch a shiver-ree [a noisy serenade given to a newly married couple] that night.

We came out to our claim the eve. before Xmas, and I don't believe a bride was ever taken to a much smaller, and queer home than I. This house is a little sod shanty 10 × 12. So first picture out the room. Now see what I've got in it. On the south end I have a door, wood box, stove, waterpail box behind the stove, and a cupboard. On the west a wash stand, chair, and window. On the north we have our bed which is a pair of springs with legs on fastened to the wall by hinges. This we let down at night, [and] strap up against the wall during the day. Have also a box where we keep our clothes, and a chair in the corner. Then on the east sits our table, a chair, slop pail, and ironing board. We have box shelves galore all around the room. Now besides all this we have an organ and stool in here, and it isn't in the middle of the room either. Can you figure out where it is? This is how we do. At night when the bed is down we push the organ up against the door, and during the day it is up against the bed. But it has to be moved every time we want to get down cellar. This small house business with large house furniture in it, isn't what its cracked up to be. Frank's mother gave us the organ before she died, and it certainly is a beauty. She died just two days before Thanksgiving.

Now I must tell you about my other house I have which will be occupied as soon as warm weather puts in its appearance. I have five nice rooms. A kitchen, dining room and sitting room down stairs, and two bedrooms upstairs. We have an open stairway going up through the dinning room. I have a nice dining table, six chairs and cupboard in the dinning room. Then I have a center table, two rockers, another chair, music cabinet and organ in the front room. There are three windows in each room and I have nice lace curtains for all. We have a lovely green iron bed, but haven't got carpets yet. This will come later. It takes oh so much [to] get started. We tried for a couple of weeks living down there and the house isn't finished off at all so the only cold weather we've had at all came then, and scared us out, so back we came to the shack. I have everything quite nice Lottie, and a nice man to go with it so would love to have you visit me any time you can. My brother Lester writes that he is coming out to see us soon. My I'll be oh so glad for no one knows how lonely it is in a new country unless they been there themselves. But everyone lives alike out here. Our new house is the largest of any around here. Nearly everyone else has shacks. Most of them you see just live the eight months [actually 14 months], prove up on it, and go back, but we're going to live the five years at the least. Then if we don't want to stay longer there will be no need of it. Mother stored all of her furniture in Anaconda, and went out in the woods to live where pa is. They are living in a little 3 room house, and she likes it very much. Lots better then she did in Anaconda. Pa is book-keeper at the mill nine miles from Florence, Mont., but they get their mail from Florence. Hows little Gladys, and your mother? I'd love so much to see you all. Just pack up and come over to my new house once for a visit.

Next Tuesday I'll be twenty-three and I know I wont feel any older than I did on Monday. Twenty-three, think of it! And as I look backward it

The homey interior of a North Dakota claim shack in Burke County, about 1900

68

seems such a short time since I was eighteen. I can remember my eigh-teenth birthday more vividly, perhaps, than any other for it was on that day I received a gift, which meant so much at that time, and a tickled and happy girl I was. Every day for five years that has been in my memory, and now another man's wife. How times, persons, and things can change in five years. Here I am with the burdens and cares of a home resting upon my shoulders, and oh pshaw, I'm just about as rattled brained as ever. Lets draw the curtain on the past, and take a peep into the future. Why dwell on things which make us unhappy. I received a letter from Mande Howe my school mate, and shes coming to visit me in July when she has her vaca-tion. Wont it be jolly. I have a dandy pony and saddle and oh such fun we will have. This is what she said tho. "Lets see, Dec., Jan., Feb., March, April, May, June, July. Gee whiz! Say let me know in time, just eight months after is a dangerous time to go visiting." Don't you think that is throwing it hard at me? I have a great deal of company, but they aren't old friends, and familiar faces after all. We had company Saturday eve, Sunday, and Mon-day. So Tuesday evening we blew out the light so they'd think we weren't at home. That's too much company isn't it? (For newlyweds any how.) Well Miss I've done well I think, and do write sooner than before. You owe me congratulations anyhow.

With lots of love to your mother, babe, and you—I'll quit now.

Lovingly, Vera, or in other words—Mrs. Frank Wintrode

Cottonwood, So. Dak.—900 miles from nowhere[48]

Claim shacks were the preferred dwelling for speculators who came to the plains only for the minimum required period (it changed over time). After this time they could "prove up" their land by paying a per-acre fee and then sell it for a profit. Sometimes these speculators' shacks were so small—often no larger than ten feet by twelve feet—that they could be built else-where and dragged to the homestead, thereby complying with the Homestead Act's house-building requirement. Arthur Joseph French, a "fourteen month man" from Minnesota who homesteaded near Crosby, North Dakota, wrote these tongue-in-cheek diary entries describing his one-room "mansion" on the prairie. He nicknamed his claim "Sunny Slope." Although his house was portable, its condition after dragging it across the prairie left much to be desired.

Preamble: "When in the course of human events" it becomes necessary for one person (composing a corporation), "in order to secure the blessings of

liberty" to himself and posterity, "do ordain," and establish residence on South 30, 163.96., for a period of fourteen months.
Dated this 17th day of March 1903

Left Portal North Dakota via the Cold Molasses Line carrying a thirty days ration, neatly packed in a cigar box, containing two lunches and three beds. Arrive at "Half Way Station," (30 miles out), at 6:30 P.M., where supper is served.

March 18. Breakfast, then to the loading platform, where my household goods and lumber for my residence (which has been laying [in] state since away last fall) is now added to my truck, which consists of a lumber wagon, drawn by a couple of Western broncos. Besides lumber, another bed, a cook stove and a chunk of lignite coal have now been added.

The mercury having reached the low point of 12 below zero (in its stocking feet), accompanied by a stiff wind, makes this trip anything but pleasant, nevertheless I reach my destination at 9:00 P.M., C.S.T. This destination is "Shady Side," my nearest neighbor, and is only twelve miles from "Sunny Slope," my objective.

March 19 to March 23. These pleasant days are spent at "Shady Side," where I am now at work constructing my residence, which will be moved later on skids to "Sunny Slope." My residence, when completed, will be a structure 10 × 12 feet, ship-lap, knot holes and tar paper. The rooms are being partitioned off by chalk marks, and consist of parlor, dining room, bath, library and kitchen, (a five room bungalo).

At 12 o'clock, noon everything being in rediness, is started off with a jerk, and a distance of nearly a mile is covered in about thirty minutes.

Here out progress is impeded with deep snow, and after hours of fruitless attempts further, said residence is left on the highest point in Williams County, to brave the elements, and said residentee is left in charge of same, and my first night at home, (the anniversary of my birthday), is spent at "Sunny Slope Inn."

March 25 to 26. At home to callers. Visitors, please ring the bell at the back door as the front door has no bell.

March 27. Again on the move, and with the setting of the sun, what is left of "Sunny Slope Inn," is hauled up and dropped. After a hasty invintory, I discover that my bath-room and Summer-kitchen have entirely disappeared, during the moving process, but being compelled to spend the night here, I again turn carpenter and set to work diligently making repairs. This completed I roll in, leaving a call for 4:00 A.M. on the morrow.

March 28. This should be written on paper of a blueish tinge, with an ideliable lead-pencil, as the condition my residence is in this morning certainly gives me a blue feeling.[49]

This Nebraska family moved their prized organ outside for a family photograph.

Busting sod with horses and a breaking plow for spring planting, about 1918

4

With Plow and Beast

While the Great Plains were once an endless landscape of grass, they have become the breadbasket for the world, having been plowed into fields and planted with row crops. Great Plains states lead the nation in the production of several varieties of wheat, as well as oats and corn. The food grown here has helped feed millions worldwide through international food programs such as Food for Peace.[50]

Today's farmers have at their disposal diesel-driven tractors that pull chisel plows easily capable of ripping open a swath of sod and soil thirty feet wide. A century and a half ago, homesteaders used a single breaking plow pulled by oxen, horses, or mules. These plows could cut open and lay over a strip of sod one foot wide, making the task difficult and time consuming. With a sharp plow and high personal resolve, a man or woman could plow one to two acres of virgin prairie sod per day. Later, huge steam-powered tractors pulled larger, more advanced plows. Whether the land was worked with animals or machines, farming was a dangerous occupation, and the prospect of a farm accident always loomed large, as it still does today.[51]

The tasks required to make the land productive were begun almost immediately after settlers arrived. Most often a lack of supplies forced them to produce their own food, as well as crops and other products for income and barter. Garden vegetables, eggs, cream, and butter were commonly traded for other food items, consumer goods, and even work. Settlers experimented with a wide variety of crops, including potatoes, rutabagas, and cabbage. Over time, they settled on two main crops that remain staples of the region—corn and wheat. They raised corn for livestock feed and wheat, a favorite among farmers, as a cash crop. Other crops included barley, oats, and flax. Farmers raised cattle, hogs, and sheep for meat as well. To provide a fresh supply of milk, cream, and butter, nearly every family kept a dairy cow—which made the journey to the homestead tied to the wagon or loaded in a boxcar.

Settlers also improved their land by planting trees—a practice evidenced by the surviving windrows today. Under the Timber Culture Act, approved by Congress in 1873, farmers who planted 40 acres of trees (later, 10 acres) and kept them growing for ten years were entitled to 160 acres of public land. The legislation reflected the nation's desire to convert the seemingly

A young family in eastern Nebraska stands next to the corn planter near their large sod house, 1880s.

barren prairie to a tree-filled paradise. Settlers also commonly planted trees and bushes around their homes to beautify their surroundings, provide shade, and raise goods such as apples. Infrequent rainfall meant that trees had to be coddled, and the daily job of hand watering them often fell to children.[52]

This tree-planting legacy has had a marked impact, not only on the appearance of the region, but on the nation's attitude toward trees. Tree lots planted under the Timber Culture Act still cast shade. The trees, now more than a hundred years old, look ancient across open stretches of prairie. Many of the slips of trees planted around homesteads also still exist, having outlived the homes and buildings they were intended to beautify and protect. When you drive across the Great Plains and see a lone stand of weathered trees, it is likely that a house once stood there. In South Dakota, remnants of "Pa's cottonwoods"—the trees that Laura Ingalls Wilder's father planted on their homestead in the 1800s near the shores of Silver Lake—are still visible. Arbor Day was officially proclaimed a state holiday in Nebraska in 1874 to help promote tree planting, and it is now celebrated nationally.

USING THE MAIL and word of mouth, settlers communicated with each other about the crop-growing potential and livabil-

ity of the various regions on the Great Plains. They trusted the judgment and insight of experienced farmers over that offered by promoters, seed salesmen, and journalists not directly engaged in farming. This bias has changed little in the region since this letter was written more than 120 years ago. Letter writer J. G. Towle was a medical doctor, a farmer, and the post-master of Towles. He wrote to encourage friends to homestead in Dakota Territory rather than attempting to farm the "sand" of western Nebraska's grass-covered sandhills. The sod crops he mentions were commonly planted and harvested the first year a settler lived on the prairie—before the land was fully plowed and prepared. Using an axe or other sharp tool to cut through the tough sod, settlers dug small holes for planting seeds that, if all went well, enabled them to feed their family and their live-stock over the first winter.[53]

Towles, Lake Co., Dak.
March 1st, 1884
Willie Wells and wife
Dear old Friends

Our girl Amelia, whom you call sister, received your welcome letter, and asks me to write some to you. You speak of going to Nebraska. Let me say to you that Nebraska is a nice country. You know I was there in 14 counties and five counties in Kansas the year before I came to Dakota, but the government lands are about all taken there, and, in fact, I found none that I could get east of Fort Kearney which is 200 miles west of the east line of the state. I came to Dakota three years last fall with Mr. Wilder. We liked it then and we still like it as will be shown by a letter we just received from him, which I will send to you to read.

I located in Lake County, the place is now called Towles, while Mr. Wilder located 60 miles north of us 12 miles west of Watertown. He located there because his daughter Emma was living there. When I first came to Towles, Lake County, the land was nearly all vacant and there was, at that time, but few settlers. The land was so near alike that there was but little choice in the pieces. The soil was a black loam, from 2 to 4 ft. deep, with a solid clay subsoil. I found that hay was abundant here, more so than further north and was worth from $2.00 to $3.00 per ton; which price it has maintained ever since; so you may know it is plenty here, or the price would be higher. We can cut hay both on the high, or cultivated land, and on the marshes, which are all remarkably smooth and level as the floor. I could start from my very door and mow a straight 100 miles if I chose. The same with breaking no stumps, no roots, but very few stone to interfere in

any way. The soil is good and it makes a fellow feel good to get good crops.
I raised this last season

> 932½ bushels of wheat
> 1,211 " " Oats
> 274 " " Barley
> 60 " " Buckwheat
> 100 " " Beggas [rutabagas]
> 125 " " Potatoes
> 60 " " Beans

Besides all kind of garden truck—except vines which was destroyed by
the gophers—and, by the way, will you please send me some melon seeds,
squash, pumpkin and cucumber seeds. Do them up in a bundle, and if you
send plenty put them in a box and send by express to J. G. Towle, Madison,
Lake County, Dakota, and I will pay the charges. Or if you can't send but a

*Farm work, including harvesting wheat, was often a family affair, as it was on the Oleson
farm in Brookings, South Dakota.*

few put them in a little pasteboard box and send by mail to Towles, Lake County, and I will remember you in my will if I don't die to quick.

Our wheat yielded from 18 to 35 bu per acre, oats 50 to 75 bu, barley 40. My buckwheat went a little over 20 bu. The first season here I planted one bag full of potatoes and got 117 bu from the one bag.

I also had this year corn enough to winter 11 hogs till next summer. Corn was injured by some by frost this year, but I will be able to save plenty seed from it. I had in 8 acres. Other years my corn all got ripe and sound. Last year I had 1,000 bushels of beggas, which cost me but little. Water is obtained by digging from 10 to 20 and 30 feet or about the same as where you are. But our wells need no curbing up for the solid clay does not cave. I dug my well in ½ day—dug 3 last fall.

You wanted to know what we burnt in Dakota. I burn, and most do in the country, hay twisted like sticks of wood or about that size, and it burns good and lasts well, about like pine wood. Six or seven loads will last a year, and in summer I would prefer it to coal or wood. But many burn coal which is here in abundance. The coal fields of Dakota, on development, will be a great source of wealth to Dakota. You can get a claim of 160 acres within the coal fields for $14 if a homestead or tree claim.

A preemption, the fee at the Land Office is $2.00 for 160 acres; this you reside on six month at the least, or 33 the most and then you pay $1.25 per acre. A homestead or tree claim costs first, on entry $14 and at time of proof of residence, etc. in six months or 5 years costs $4.00 more, making $18.00 for 160 acres. Is this cheap enough for you? If so, pull up stakes and come to Dakota as soon as you can. You can get plenty of land to put to crops of wheat and oats, then you can commence to break on your own claim and sow it to flax, right on the sod as fast as broken, and that is all till you cut your flax which is done with a machine similar to wheat or oats, and you get a yield of from 10 to 15 bushels per acre, and it is now worth $1.50 per bu. This makes a return of $15.00 per acre from your own Dakota farm the first year so you don't have to wait a year or two for a crop. Two large or three midling sized horses will break from 2 to 3 acres per day—week out and week in, from April 15 to July 15, or three months, or 90 days. So you see you can open quite a farm in a short time if you choose—and raise a crop on all of it consisting of flax, beans, potatoes, yes, yes, potatoes right on sod, dropped and plowed under, sod corn and beggas.

We are not required to build fences—therefore you will see none on coming to this pleasant country and is a great relief to a poor man, and our crops are not in the least injured by stock, etc. for the herd law is strictly in force here. Irvin had a herd of cattle last summer, 152 head which he got $152 or a dollar a head, for herding from May 1st to October 1st.

The summer before he also had a herd. It is not much bother to take care of them. Several new railroads are being built in Dakota. In fact, they push right out ahead of the settlement where the land is all vacant yet, knowing that in a single season, emigration will flock in and fill up the space. (We have no indians except on their reservations west of the Missouri river. See map I sent to you.) I think I sent you a book about our land, if not please write me and I will give you all the information I can. Ask any questions you see fit and you will receive a prompt reply from me. When you are about ready to start, write me and I will tell you where to land here. New comers are arriving here to get a slice of Uncle Sam's domain. And "what other folks can do, why with patience can not you." Only keep this rule in view, come to Dakota and begin anew.

You ask if there is any vacant land yet in Dakota. Yes, thousands of acres, as yet unsurveyed. They can not survey it as fast as it is taken up, and many have gone 50 and 60 miles ahead of the survey—so as to be there to grab as soon as surveyed.

The lay of the country is, generally, slightly rolling about like Lemonweir Prairie, while in many places it is as level as a barn floor for miles, with houses dotted here and there. I can count 50 houses from my door. This fall I built a fine frame house 24 by 34 feet with chamber in the whole of it, and the porch the same as I had on the place where I lived there, with a good cellar etc. It cost me $800 now and it is not yet plastered. It will have 6 rooms below, 8 above.

We keep the post office stationary etc. Amelia is as happy as a lark and is well pleased with it here. She is a right good girl. Is industrious and will take a claim with you and is anxious for you to come. She got a letter from her cousin Frank in Dakota. He is with Mell Davis 40 miles east of here.

You ask the price of deeded land here. A deeded quarter consisting of 160 acres is worth from $1,000 to $1,600 or about $10 per acre. Some pieces bring as high as $ three thousand dollars—according to the amount of improvements. Tell Albert Towle I have just been to see Jake Walker. He has given up the hotel business, and bought a farm for three thousand dollars and is doing well. He laughs about you fellows on the sand.

J. G. Towle, P.M.[54]

SETTLERS OFTEN POOLED RESOURCES and tasks such as plowing and planting to help each other get established as quickly as possible. Sometimes—as in the following case—they would farm adjoining tracts of land and even live together until the work of setting up the farm was done. The author of this letter, Lewellyn Amos Gushee, was a veteran of the Union army's 13th Massachusetts Volunteers. He had taught school in

West Virginia and Ohio prior to becoming a successful home-steader in Nebraska.

Lincoln Lancaster Nebraska
June 5, 1873
Dear Mother:

I have time to write a few lines while waiting for a train. Hills and I homesteaded each 160 acres joining in Polk Co Neb. 3½ miles from Osceala, the Co Seat, and our P.O. address, 38 miles from the Seward R[ail]R[oad] terminus of the Midland Pacific, 25 miles from Columbus. [I] can see over 40 houses from my shanty besides (Osceala). I have got 15 acres broken & about 5 acres sod corn planted, also beans, potatoes & forest tree seeds, have got a well of excellent water only 146 feet deep, bored with an eleven in. auger. Bought me a splendid Roan mare at a bargain 115 dollars; people say she is worth 150. I rode her yesterday to Seward 38 ms & came here this forenoon 26 ms on [railroad] cars and entered another 160 acres under the Timber Culture Act of Mar 3, 1873. I am obligated to plant 40 acres of timber in 1 year in order to hold it, so I shall have my hands full for awhile unless I can get some of you to come on and take it off my hands (George, or Frank say) but I have just heard that Abner Harwood had a letter stating that they had come out West to his brother's, Nehemiah Pease. I suppose I wrote to Frank when I was here the first time to homestead and if he read my letter before he started, shall expect a call from them.

I have got the regular Nebraska appetite, could eat anything from raw dog to army mules, so my health is good of course. There are three of us living together in a 12x12 shanty, Hills and a man with a team breaking for us. Hills does the cooking. He wants to enter a 160 under the TC Act and have his boy come live on it, Amelia also if she chooses. We are both well suited with our selections; there is a nice RR Sec joining mine that can be bought for 4½ an acre. This is a beautiful and healthful country setting up very rapidly and just as nice lands as can be found any where. I cannot homestead for you but I can turn over this 160 that I have just entered to you if you wish to come out. I don't think I shall send for Mary till Fall. I think women better not come until a decent place is provided for them to live in. Perhaps you and Martha would like to come out with her—write and let me know what you think about it—By the way has Martha got home from Mass yet? Would like to hear from her. Saw all the folks in Schuyler I knew when I passed through there.

L. A. Gushee[55]

THE DAY-TO-DAY WORKLOAD and drudgery of farming the land is detailed in the diary of John Alfred Borg, a Swedish immigrant to Nebraska. Like many farmers, the only day he took off from farming and selling or trading his produce was Sunday, enabling him to attend church and visit with neighbors.

July (1897)

I. Cultivated

II. Cultivated

III. Cultivated. To Allen for July 4th celebration. Traded butter for various items, $1.08.

IV. Sunday. To church. Dennisons, Warns, and Holmbergs visited us.

V. Cultivated.

VI. Cultivated.

VII. Cultivated.

VIII. To Wakefield. Sold a ram for $3.42. Traded butter for various items, $1.70.

IX. Cultivated. Hauled corn for Swan Swanson 2 loads. Bought 3 loads of corn 150 bushels from August Lincoln for $8.00. To pay when I can.

X. To Wakfield. Borrowed and sent my brother $187.50. Arranged loan on the steers $1,050.00 for 8 months to Haskell. Traded butter, 88 cents. Sold a pig to Morgan, $2.00. Rained at night.

XI. Sunday, visited Charley Fransons. Nice weather.

XII. Cultivated corn. Hiram Jones came for a load of hay, $1.00.

XIII. Cultivated corn.

XIV. Cultivated corn.

XV. To Allen. Traded butter for various items, $2.45.

XVI. Cultivated.

XVII. Cultivated.

XVIII. Sunday to church and to Helgrens.

XIX. Cultivated.

XX. Rained. To Wakefield. Traded eggs and butter, $3.50 for various items.

XXI. Cultivated. August Helgrens and Jon Lennarts were here.

XXII. Cultivated.

XXIII. Cultivated.

XXIV. Cultivated. Alfred went to Allen with butter, $1.76.

XXV. To church. A. L. Olsons and Andrew Johnsons visited us. Received for hay land $7.00 rent from Peter Olson. Received from A. L. Olson for seed corn 50 cents.

XXVI. Finished cultivating the corn. To Allen with 4 hogs—got $2.20. It came to $38.13.[56]

UNDER THE HOMESTEAD ACT, single women who were at least twenty-one years of age could file and claim land. Many women took advantage of the opportunity, including Alice Newberry, a Colorado schoolteacher. Depending on the state and time period, single women probably made up from 5 to 20 percent of all homesteaders. Many women built their own houses and farmed the land themselves. Others, like Ms. Newberry, entered into a financial agreement with a neighbor to farm her land in exchange for a share of the harvest, an arrangement male homesteaders often made as well. Newberry tells her mother that her experiences feeding the hired hand— "the man with the plow"—have convinced her to study for a calling higher than marriage.[57]

Stratton, Colorado
June 4, 1907
Dear Mama:

When I wrote you about a month ago, I did not tell you that I have a boarder. I didn't have him then, I believe. He is putting in the crop on my

A smiling South Dakota woman tends her spacious garden

farm. Mr. Wellman furnishes the team and man and the seed and farming implements, and is farming my land. I have to have so much land tilled in order to prove up. Breaking costs $2.00 for every acre broken. This way it costs me nothing but the month's board and bother of having the man. He is a very good, mild, meek, patient, respectable married man from North Dakota, and faithful in his work. There was no one else to board him, because by the time he drove the team back and forth from Wellman's here—ten miles—the remainder of the day would not count for much, and any way he is slow. Then it would be too hard on the horses and breaking the sod seems to tire them very much as it is. Mr. Wellman will have the crop. This is the way they always bargain on new land the first year. I am glad to get the work done in this way. I hope Mr. W. won't be hailed out [destroyed by hail] as he was on his own place last year.

I am sure there never was a man who ate so much as "Henry." He is very nice to cook for because he eats all of my experiments without a murmur. But there is usually very little left over to warm up in the way of potatoes. He will get through this week, and I know it's wicked, but I want to say, "Praise the Lord." I wouldn't be married for anything, not to a man who eats so much. It takes all my time to cook, and when I am through there is very little to show for it except a remark that he made once that he used to weigh one hundred seventy-five, and last time he was weighed it was two-hundred ten. That is solid comfort, but I can't claim all the glory and renown for the extra thirty five pounds because Mrs. Wellman had him two months before I acquired him. Then too he seemed to think part of the gain in weight due to a heavy fur coat which he wore when he was weighed. This seems to me base ingratitude.

He is very slow. It takes him more than an hour to get ready to come in from the field, wash his hands and face, after feeding the team, comb his hair, and plod from the little shanty Mr. Wellman built for him and which is not ten rods from the dugout. Finally, he gets in to the table. Our conversation is limited to my asking him if he will have some of this or that, and to his saying "Please" or merely taking the dish without saying anything. After his hunger is partly satisfied he may talk about corn or rain. He is almost worse than "the man with the hoe," he is a "man with the plow." A hoe does require some intellect in its use. You must be careful how and where you use it. The plow, once your furrow is started straight, will almost go of itself, and there are clods and grass roots, always. Oh I know Van Dyke writes of "grass, and the smell of fresh new earth," but these men who go on day after day and year after year, with it seems to me nothing to look forward to, and hope for, inspire my respect—I was going to say veneration. There is something about them that I have not in my make-up, the power to plod, plod, plod.

When he is so slow I feel like throwing things, and I have all I can do sometimes not to say things.

Yesterday was a very exciting meal for us, that is for me. My table as I have remarked before stands close to the wall. He stopped eating, not suddenly, of course, and stared at the wall near him as if fascinated. It is unusual for him to stop eating and I was on the [alert] at once. "What do you see" I said, "a centipede?" " No," he said slowly, "it was a worm." I looked at the wall but the thing had vanished. "What sort of worm?" I demanded. "A brown worm with a lot of legs." "It was a centipede," I told him. I impolitely yanked the table from the wall, but the "worm" was nowhere to be seen. "It went just as quick" he said. "Yes," I said hotly, "they go like lightening." I expatiated on their being poisonous. He seemed interested for he asked if their bite would kill one. I wanted to tell him "Yes, always," but I was afraid the worm might play Nemesis in the night and sting me. So I was truthful. He went on eating. That is the first centipede I have known of in here. This morning I killed one outside.

I have decided not to marry. Three warm meals a day, three-hundred-sixty-five days in the year for the term of my natural life is more than I can face. I have decided to study up a little and try to fit myself for a higher calling. Please look among the books at home and send my Latin grammar—the "Allece and Greenough." It must be there for it isn't here. I enclose postage and Florence's letter.

I presume Edna is at home now. I plan to write to her when the man has left me.

With love to all

Alice[58]

THE VAST SIZE *of the Great Plains meant that settlement and homesteading often extended for more than one generation. This was the case for one new, turn-of-the-century settler and her brother, whose father had homesteaded in Minnesota in 1878. While there were similarities—such as burning buffalo chips for fuel—the differences between the generations were substantial. Mechanized farm equipment had replaced the horse-driven plow, people traveled by trains instead of wagons, and typewritten letters had replaced handwritten notes. Even annual precipitation levels were very different, as Ilma Cale points out to her father. Homesteaders settling on the western side of the Great Plains during the early twentieth century experienced far less moisture on average than those from the previous generation who settled farther east. Not only did this*

impact crops and gardens, but it meant a lack of surface water.
Settlers often had to haul their water a mile or more from
streams and muddy, mosquito-infested sloughs, or collect it
when it rained.

Ilma, a schoolteacher by training, and her brother Max
successfully homesteaded land in eastern Colorado, despite the
challenges posed by inadequate water. Today, much of the land
broken on the western Great Plains during the settlement era
has been returned to pasture for grazing and to production of
hay because it was unsuitable for raising most crops.

Wild Horse, Colorado, May 24, 1908
Dear Papa:

Your letter of the 21st reached me last night. Mr. Klein went to town, as he always does on Saturday, and he brought it out with him. Thanks for the [bank] draft, and I hope it didn't bother you any.

Yes, I suppose this homesteading reminds you and Mamma of the early days in Bloom [Minnesota]. It makes me think of them too. The prairie out here looks very much as it did in Bloom, or will when the grass gets a good start. So far there has been so little rain that grass has not done much except in the draws [coulees]. However, this week it has been threatening to rain nearly every day, and last night the weather got down to business and it rained all night. We must have got a little more than two inches and the ground is pretty well soaked. It cleared off in the morning but began to rain again about two o'clock and is still raining. Think it must have rained at least half an inch this afternoon for it came very hard for an hour or so. We expect that everything will start now and we will put in a lot of beans and such things. I hope it is not too late for the potatoes that were planted some time ago. Max put them in on rather high ground because that was about all he could get broken up before it got so dry that they could not break at all. They would have had a much better chance if he had put them on lower ground, I think, but they may be all right even yet. I hardly think it will get so dry again for all the old settlers say that it has been an unusually dry spring. There is something peculiar about the soil here. It doesn't seem to absorb the water very readily even though it is rather sandy. We walked across the prairie last night after it had been raining half an hour, and the water was standing in little pools all over the ground. One would think that it would soak right in when the soil is so dry, but it don't. There are little pools standing all over the prairie now and the water holes down in the draw are full, of course. Last night Max put the tub and some pails under the eves and caught a lot of soft water and this morning he scooped up a big barrel full from some of the pools that are standing around. It is nice to have real soft water though the well water here is not so very hard. We can use soap in it all right and it is nothing like the hard water in Minnesota.

It has stopped raining just now and I am going to go out and sow some of the blue grass seed that Mamma sent out. I think I can scatter a few handfuls around my house and it ought to come up all right. Tomorrow we will put in more garden, for Roberts has promised to break a little piece for me. He is delighted about the rain and expects to get quite a field put in this week. Suppose he will plant corn and cane and perhaps alfalfa. I bought some alfalfa seeds myself and will seed a little around Max's house so the hens can have some.

Max and I and Roberts are keeping house alone now, for the Kleins have moved down into their shack. It was a great relief to have them go. Of course they were lots of company but the shack and they made such a lot of extra work. Agnes is a good cook but she does everything the very hardest way and she liked to be busy practically all day long just with the cooking. I get it all done up in half the time and could even if I had half a dozen boarders. It is funny how some women make hard work of things. Even Max notices that I do the work much easier than Agnes and I did when we worked together. She used to use every single dish in the house when she made a pie or two or a pudding, and on the whole her cooking didn't turn out a bit better than mine. She got so she could make good bread. I have made only one batch myself and it was not such a great success. It didn't rise well and that is always the difficulty because the nights here are so cold and we have no very good way of keeping it warm. Roberts always wraps his big fur coat around the bread pan, and that helps a good deal, but still it doesn't rise at night as it ought to. Think I will have to set it out so that it will rise in the daytime. Agnes does it that way now, and it works much better.

Tell Mamma I can get along all right without the gem [muffin] pans if they have not been sent already. I find that gems are just as nice when I bake them in a pie tin. I made some dandy gems the other day and Max and Roberts didn't leave a crumb of them. Those two eat as much as our whole family at home, so the cooking is quite a job even when I only have to cook for us three.

It is too bad you have too much rain but we people out here on the plains can't understand how that can be. We think there couldn't be too much rain anywhere, so, you see, it all depends on the point of view. However, we have great hopes now that there will be enough rain so we can raise things this summer. It has been so chilly that nothing has done very well even where it was irrigated in the garden, but radishes and such things are up nicely anyhow. There have only been one or two real warm days since we came out. It is generally quite warm for a while in the middle of the day and then at four o'clock it gets very chilly and is cold all night.

Max and Roberts have been busy hauling loads of buffalo chips in. It makes first rate fuel, fully as good as the soft coal we get out here, and Roberts says it is the same as the lignite coal they get in North Dakota. I think he is mistaken but he has been up there a good deal and ought to know. I have learned how to regulate the stove and can get along with it nicely now.

Max will fix up that plat Mamma wanted and send it to her. He has been all over this section and has a good memory for the lay of the land. He seems to feel very cheerful about the deal most of the time and thinks it

Steam-powered tractors began to replace animals for some of the backbreaking farm work after 1900.

will turn out well. If things get a good start now he is almost certain to sell some more land. Roberts expects two friends of his to come out in about a month. I think they will take homesteads up near his claim.

Yesterday the boys were shooting at an antelope but did not get it. It followed the wagon for quite a while and came up pretty close. Roberts shot several times but I guess he is not such a good shot. He got a duck last week and we had it for dinner.

Have to mail this now. Will write more later.

Ilma[59]

A young woman gathering wildflowers near an isolated tar-paper shack

5

The Menace from Within

The Great Plains can be a lonely place. Today in some western counties, the population averages four people or less per square mile. Not unexpectedly, this remoteness has created a unique sense of neighborliness and camaraderie, even among people who have never met each other. Strangers can strike up a conversation almost anywhere with anyone, causing several plains states to promote themselves as being home to the "friendliest" people in America.[60]

One hundred or more years ago this feeling of isolation was amplified. Settlers found that the excitement of arriving and living in an exotic place was quickly replaced by a sense of loneliness and homesickness. Even if crops were growing and the homestead a success, settlers, especially those on the forefront of the wave of migration, often lived alone on the vast, treeless prairie. Others were surrounded by just a handful of distant neighbors, some of whom didn't even share their language.

In the essay "Between Earth and Sky," Debra Marquart tells the story of her German Russian ancestors arriving on the North Dakota prairie in 1885. While her great-grandfather saw untold economic opportunities before him, her great-grandmother fell to her knees and cried out, "Das ist der Himmel auf Erde!" which translated roughly means, "It's all earth and sky!" Her reaction was common.[61]

Surrounded by little more than grass, many settlers deeply missed their friends, their families, and the amenities of the regions they came from. They longed for social opportunities, their former close-knit communities, and conversation partners. Loneliness and homesickness became worse when heads of households were forced to find work elsewhere to make ends meet, or when a member of the family died. In the winter, when snow prevented trains and mail from arriving, months passed without word from family members or the rest of the outside world.

Sitting alone in a shack or a sod house, with the ever-present wind roaring in their ears, was too much for some homesteaders. Emotional breakdowns were not uncommon, and loneliness and isolation ranked with drought and grasshoppers as factors that drove settlers off the Great Plains. A booklet proclaiming the virtues of Dakota Territory to would-be settlers offered a perhaps unintended twist on the promotional efforts of the region's boosters when it featured a sketch of the new "Insane Asylum" in Yankton immediately adjacent to the new statehouse in Bismarck.[62]

IN THIS EARLY LETTER, Harriett Carr writes poetically about both the Kansas prairie and her parents' home in Massachusetts. Settlers like Carr, whose husband Benjamin operated a new store in Lawrence, Kansas, were often torn emotionally about moving onto the Great Plains. Though struck by the raw beauty of the prairie and the economic opportunities available to them, they desperately missed their old homes, family, friends, and the relative ease of living in populated areas of the eastern United States. They longed for any information from back home, including letters and newspapers—even if they were months old.

Lawrence [Kansas] Jul. 4th 1858
Dear Father + Mother

As Benjamin is writing to you to night I thought that perhaps a few lines from me might also be acceptable And a few they will have to be for the evenings are of no length now and it is about bed time; I wrote a long time since but the letter lies yet in my portfolio from neglect to send it. This is a very beautiful evening. Our vast prairie looks soft and green rolling far far away in the distance and the bright waters of our noble river sparkle in the red twilight tints while the dark green forests that line its banks lie like some beauteous picture against the clear sky. I think the trees and grass have such a deep bright tint of green here—much more so than in the East. It may be owing to the frequent showers we have had in part—but I think the principal cause is in some property in the soil. This brightness of color helps very much to increase the wonderful beauty of this unrivalled land.

It certainly is the most beautiful country my eyes ever beheld—but still no spot on this Earth seems so sweet and home like as your hills with their white villages clustered in their sheltered nooks. I love old Massachusetts and if ever we are able to do so, I mean that there shall be my home. The prairie is vast, magnificent and grand—but we miss the dear old trees, the gardens, the flowers and birds those pleasing and home like scenes which make the heart soft and happy. Oh how I long for such a home—for a little cot with the grand elms waving over it and the birds singing their joyous anthems amid the branches. I never could be contented to call this land my home beautiful though it may be. I wake oft times on a Sabbath morn as the sun shines brightly through my window and listen to the clamour, drunkenness and awful profanity which we hear in these streets. And then I think of the sweet quiet home of my youth—the cool pleasant parlor—the fresh morning air scented with the fragrance of the blooming fruit trees or the garden flowers—stealing in at the open windows—the dear brother and sisters strolling in the garden or reading in the shade and the white haired kind father with the Bible on his knee and my heart grows sick with longings and my eyes dim with tears.

Yesterday the 4th was celebrated here in the shape of a picnic over the river in the woods and a company of "Antiques and Horribles" [unofficial celebrants] parading the street. Of course you have heard of the affair of Lane and Jenkins which has caused such an excitement here. Lane has had his examination before Justin Ladd and acquitted, but Benjamin says he has written about it so I will say no more. Probably he has written about our moving too—We are now on the main street living in a room over his store. I don't like to live in a town but I must make the best of it. We got Mothers and Hatties letter; I never received the letter she sent to Ogden else I should have answered it; I mean to write to her before long. I must close now with love to all and a request that you write as soon as possible. We get no letters more welcome than yours dear Father and Mother so deny them not to us.

Truly your daughter

Harriett

The business of men being necessarily more rough here than in the East, rough clothes are quite allowable. There are nice carriages here, nice horses but the riders in carriages and in ox carts are neither above or below the other. Society is much more on a level here than at the east.

We had a smirk at O Wileys expense to day. Mrs Kelsey wrote that she was delighted with the beauty of Kansas especially Leavenworth. Leavenworth is a busy fast growing town situated on the Missouri River among the woods. Leavenworth is the same in appearance as any young town—as yet not very big outbuildings generally—rather dirty streets etc but if ever you come to Kansas don't look for its glorious and unrivalled beauty in Leavenworth but go out on these great magnificent green praries rolling far far away in the soft blue distance intersected over and over by long narrow belts of trees which mark the course of some river or stream—this great ocean with its bright green grassy billows is the beauty of Kansas and not Leavenworths dirty streets. Leavenworth truly looks very pretty situated quite romantically as you look at it from a little distance, but it has no connection with the famed beauty of the land. . . . It is the great upheaval mass of Earth branded with the storms of long ages and whose aerial shores seem dyed with the deeps of Heaven that thrill the soul with gazing at the old mountain and not the tiny work of mans hand that mars its grand solitude. It is the land as Nature formed it and painted with her brightest green that delights the eye and feast the soul here in Kansas and not the cobwebs of mans invention which has begun to dot its hitherto silent and uninhabited glory.

It is getting dusk and I must draw this to a close at least for tonight for it is a sin to write when such a fresh shower has made air and Earth so fragrant—

Monday noon

I will do this up and put it in the Office with love to all the folks and a request that you serve me better than I have you. We are going to have fresh oysters for dinner preserved in air tight cans the same as fruit. Tell Mrs. Kelsey I will answer soon

Harriett[63]

SOME SETTLERS KEPT DIARIES, mostly matter-of-fact records of weather, crops, chores, and occasional visitors. On one gloomy day in 1869, Ella Bailey could muster energy for only a short, plaintive comment on her new life on the plains.

April 8, 1869

Been thinking of home. I can't help but wish I had never seen Colorado. It is lonesome and desolate. If being here didn't make one think of home, I don't know what would.

Ella Bailey

Latham, Weld County, Colorado[64]

OCCASIONAL LETTERS FROM CHILDREN suggest the concerns of the young. The author of this letter, a boy aged nine or ten, lived in a sod house near Olivet, Dakota Territory, with his father and stepmother. They struggled to make a living farming and burned buffalo chips, or dried manure, in the winter to stay warm. The letter is remarkably well written for a boy of his time period—a testament to the fact that his father had been a schoolteacher and that life on the prairie often made children wise beyond their years. (Daniel's mother died while giving birth to his younger brother Thomas, who died eight months later.) Daniel wrote this letter to his maternal grandmother, whom he clearly missed. He eventually moved off his father's homestead into town, going to work in the watch repair business.

Olivet, Dakota

Hutchison Co

Nov 4th [1880?]

My dear Grandma,

Perhaps you have forgotten there is such a boy in the world as Daniel Demorest Sharp, but its a fact. and I am that boy and you are my Grand-

A detailed tally of letters written and received, as recorded in a young woman's diary

Ma. I thought I would write and mention it before it was too late for if I neglect much longer that boy will be something else. Well Grandma how do you do any way, it seems so long since I saw you or heard of you that I hardly know what to write about. I hope you are enjoying good health and feel happy. I should like to see you and talk with you but of course that is impossible. I am not sure this letter will find you but I hope it will.

Since you were here we have had pretty fair health and some sickness. I have had most of the health, and papa and [step]mamma the best share of the rest. I believe papa must be getting old; he has had so much rheumatism. Now he dont have it all. I have some myself sometimes. Last spring Olivet and I took a start at growing. My trousers are getting to short and

Olivet is spreading around considerable. Mr. White built a new store, there is a fine Milwaukee Courthouse, two new hotels. Norrie Baldwin has built a church and the Cambellites are going too, and the Devil has got as many as both put together as any body can have Dutch beer or Kentuckey whiskey as they like. There are a good many houses built, too. I could tell you plenty of news, but it would be of folks you dont know. I dont hear much from Uncle Fraileigh, Grandpa Sharp wrote us some about Barrington people last spring, and Uncle Dan has forgot me I guess. I suppose he has plenty of boys and girls of his own to think about. I intend writing to him too as soon as I can. If you are at Aunt Katy's please give my love to her and Uncle Asbury and to my cousins Charley and George. I suppose Charley is about man grown by now. Maybe I shall be able to go and see you all some day. I should like to very much.

We are just getting into the beginning of winter though we have only had light frosts so far. I am going to trap for furs this winter when it freezes up. I made some money at it last year and can do better this. But I shall also attend school, we have a fine house and a good attendance. This is the pleasantest fall I have seen in Dakota—very little frost yet. We dont expect a hard winter. Times pretty hard, a great many people wont be able to meet their debts, wheat only 50 cts. Come and see the roan heiffer, she is as big as the old cow. But I also want you to come and see me too, and stay and visit when you are here. I shall be mad if Mitchell gets you and hides you away next time. We have 15 head of cattle and horses; now it takes about 55 acres of hay to winter our stock. We expect seven calves next spring. Papa says I may also say "and a lot of chickens that are not hatched." He says he can manage to keep poor by hard work. Claims are worth from $800 to $2000 round here now. I think ours worth $1600 and in two years it will be worth $2500. Papa has not run in debt or mortgaged yet and I hope he never will.

Bet you I'm tired Grandma. I am not used to writing. You must not get provoked at my bad writing. You know I love you. I always did and always shall. I send my best love to you. Papa and mamma join me. Please write to me when you can.

I remain your Loving Grandson,

Daniel Sharp[65]

THE SUDDEN APPEARANCE OF NEIGHBORS—even if they were two miles or more away—was cherished by settlers, especially by those who had children needing companions. As Caroline Larrabee points out, however, isolation was often only temporary. In most locations development came quickly in the form of 160-acre farmsteads—especially after a railroad laid track into a nearby area.

Dakota Terr'y 1882

Dear Patty

At last we have a real, bona-fide settler. He has taken a pre-emption on the south side of Lake Belland and is building him a "wee brown soddy." He is working for Mr. Larrabee and will move his family here. His name is Geo. Bakken. My, it seems so comfy to have some woman near even if she is a couple of miles away. These people have some family and I am glad for the sakes of our family for our children will have some other children to play with.

It was a real fact about the R.R. and it has come in as far as Jamestown. Another townsite is platted in this county and is called Carrington after Henry Carrington of Toledo, Ohio, of the Carrington Casey Land Co. This will bring in the settlers and soon we will see a shack on every quarter section. You may wonder what a quarter section is. It is 160 acres of land ½ a mile long and all the land is surveyed in that way here

The mail now instead of coming from Jamestown comes via Carrington and a P.O. has been established here with Mr. Larrabee as Post Master.

Caroline H. [Larrabee][66]

THE NEXT LETTER'S AUTHOR, a member of a homestead colony's land-locating committee, has come to Colorado to start a new life and make his fortune. Unfortunately for him, the woman he loves has stopped writing him, making his life "among strangers" miserable. Obviously, she does not share in his enthusiasm for trading her life in Michigan City, Michigan, for that of a cattle rancher's wife on the Colorado plains. Would-be marriage partners and spouses alike commonly balked at the notion of moving onto the distant plains and struggling to carve out a life there.

Greely Col. July 10th 1871

My Dear Rhoda

I have the blues tonight about as bad as a man can have them. I came from Cheyenne today and was feeling very bad because I had not heard from you since I came out here. I found a letter here from you but it did not raise my spirits much. You seem to censure me because I did not remain in the [illegible.]

Now Rhoda I know you would not do so if you knew my motives in doing so. I will tell you it was my great love for you and my strong desire to make a pleasant home for you together with a desire to get out of the worse set of men it was ever my misfortune to be oblige to mix with in my life. I was appointed one of the locating committee of the Milwaukee Colony and thinking I would never have a better chance to see this western country and not cost me a cent so I accepted the appointment and am here on that business. I have seen a great deal of this wonderfull country and will see more before I return if return I ever do. Rhoda, I did go to Mich City and would have went to see you if I possibly could have done so. I went there on business connected with the colony and returned to Milwaukee as soon as I had transacted all of my business.

In some respects I like Colorado very much The climate is delightful and the natural scenery in and about the Rocky Mountains is unequaled in the United States and I feel satisfied that I could easily make myself independent in five years out here by hard work and economy in raising stock. It is the best paying business in Colorado and requires the least labor and the person that goes into it to make money must live rough for a couple of years. But I can commence here with $1000 and in five years clear $15000 and that is more than a man can do in the states with that amt of capital. Stock requires no food either winter or summer and the cost per head to keep them here $1.50 a year.

I am satisfied Rhoda you would never be willing to come out here to live and for that reason I have abandoned the idea myself. I cannot live here unless you are with me. You did not tell me what you thought of my going to New Carlisle in with Hiram Humphrey in the Hard Ware business. Would you like to live there? I would make a strong effort to get into and remain in any business or locality that would please the only woman on earth that I truly love if you would tell me. I can't ask you to come out here and live as we would be oblidge to if I went into the stock business for money. If we could live in a nice little town like this, it would be all right but there is nothing here that would pay. A man can't live on climate or beautiful scenery alone. This will be one of the prettiest places in the west before many years. It lies within plain sight on the Denver Pacific R.R. 50 miles from Denver. Longs Peak looms up in the distance and the Snow Range can be seen at all times from the Hotel where I am staying. I saw plenty of Buffalo coming across the Plains. But it is nothing new to you since you have been over this ground long before I was. I don't know when I get through out here. I would like to see Mr. Reynolds and talk with him. I see he has more influence with you than I have and I think I could get an opinion from him.

I hope you had a pleasant time the 4th at Mich City. I was in Denver and spent a misserable day out here among strangers. I thought of you many times during the day and looked long and anxiously for a letter but none came. I rec'd one from Mary at Denver but that did not satisfy me. I wanted to hear from Rhoda and did expect to find a letter for me when I came then but none. Then days passed and I had ceased to look for a letter from you. Rhoda it is cruel in you to be so unmindful of my feelings. I love you with my whole love and cannot bear to be neglected in that manner.

There is not an hour of my life but some portion of it is devoted to thoughts of you and plans for your future happiness but I fear you do not feel the same towards me. I will not annoy you with this kind of talk any more. I fear I have already made my letter too long for you but I felt just like writing tonight. Every person in the house has gone to bed but me and it is still as death, not a sound to be heard.

Remember me to Mr. R. and also Mr. James Reynolds Family. I would like to hear from you often Rhoda while I am out here so if you will write promptly this time you can direct to Denver. I will be there again before long and will look for a letter from you. Be sure you will always get a prompt ans. from me. It is after twelve and I will close so good night Darling.

I remain your devoted Geo.[67]

A pensive North Dakota homesteader in the doorway of her wind-blown claim shack

A sun-tanned Nebraska couple, their three very young children, and two optimistically planted trees

Mothers and young children on the prairie, Lone Tree, Nebraska

6

Families of the Prairie

Many stories of families who settled on the Great Plains have found their way into print, allowing readers today to share in the experience. Willa Cather's novels *O! Pioneers* and *My Ántonia* grew out of her family's move from Virginia to an unsuccessful homestead near Red Cloud, Nebraska, when she was nine. O. E. Rølvaag's classic novel *Giants in the Earth*—the story of Norwegians who joined the "great settling" and struggled to survive on the prairie—was based, in part, on the accounts told to him by his wife and in-laws, who had been homesteaders in eastern South Dakota.

After hearing her mother, Laura Ingalls Wilder, tell stories of growing up in the Midwest and Great Plains, Rose Wilder Lane encouraged her to write down stories of her life as a young girl and young woman. At the age of sixty-three, she agreed, and over the next dozen years Wilder produced seven books that help children around the world understand what it was like to live in sod dugouts and experience the joys and hardships of a childhood on the plains.

During the settlement era, children were almost as abundant as shucks of wheat. The opportunities land ownership provided young adults setting out in life, coupled with the hard work associated with staking out land claims and farming, meant that most settlers and homesteaders were in their twenties and thirties. Many of them arrived accompanied by young children or began families once their farms and businesses were established.[68]

Born and raised in sod houses and claim shacks, children lived extraordinary lives. With hats and sunbonnets in tow, they roamed and played games in fields while their parents worked nearby. They picked up buffalo bones amidst the grass and watched intently as American Indians traversed across their farms. With their families, they celebrated and socialized, attended dances, held picnics in the summer, swam in sloughs and creeks, and went sledding in the winter.

Once an area became developed, children walked or rode horses to one-room sod or tar-paper schools, sometimes accompanied by their parents and sometimes alone. They studied literature, math, history, geography, and grammar in buildings heated in the winter by a stove that burned whatever fuel happened to be available—wood, coal, twisted hay, or buffalo chips. Teachers were frequently fellow homesteaders and settlers, many of whom were graduates of teacher's colleges and had journeyed west to stake out their own land claims. While some students left school after attending a few grades to work on the farm, many stayed and completed their educations. A number went on to college to become teachers themselves or excelled in other areas. (William McKnight, who was born in a sod house in South Dakota, went on to lead the 3M Corporation for more than thirty years.)[69]

If the children of settlers lived on a farm, they took on many of the plentiful daily tasks as they grew older—watering trees, working in gardens, feeding livestock, and helping with the kitchen chores. When the landholdings of successful farmers grew, children frequently became integral parts of a successful farm or ranch.

FOR IMMIGRANT SETTLERS, the birth of a child on a claim or homestead was an important event. A child born in America came to signify the completion of the journey that began with their voyage across the ocean. The Norwegian immigrant who wrote the following letter found satisfaction in his growing family that helped offset the economic struggles experienced on his farm. Though he kept careful track of what was occurring in his homeland, and even retained his preference for traditional clothing, his ties to the old country began to fade as his children and grandchildren became Americanized through life on the Great Plains.

Luverne, Mn.
March 13, 1875
Dear Parents and Siblings,

As I have special news to tell you I can wait no longer to write a letter—have neglected it too long already. Just four weeks ago, on February 13, Anna gave birth to a fine baby girl. On February 28 the child was baptized and given the name Astrid. She is thriving well and is a beautiful baby. Anna is also doing very well, so I have much for which to thank God.

Little Sigri is a plump, active little girl, talks quite well and rocks her baby sister in the cradle, but is not mature enough to qualify as baby sitter yet. The little boys are all fine and Niels is of great help to me. I am so very pleased with my children—they are my only kingdom and a wonderful link between myself and the present times. I am often very tired and yearn for eternal rest where all troubles must disappear; but I have all these little ones to live for, and to raise as good citizens wherever they go. This is a great responsibility and much hard work. But the heaviness is lifted from that load when our lord adds His blessing, giving the harvest such as I experience daily with my family. Such a shame that I never get a good

A family wearing Sunday-best clothes poses in the shade by a stream near their sod house, Custer County, Nebraska, 1887.

photo of them to send to you. Then you would see for yourself that they are well equipped in both body and soul. Yet I am determined that neither the family or myself wish to again be disfigured by an unqualified photographer.

As my family increases, my herd of animals is decreasing—as a result of some bad years. It has been necessary to sell or butcher some cattle as the family might require. But, praise God, we have not yet suffered any starvation. As one man expressed the situation, "It is the almighty bushel of wheat that should take care of everything," and when that fails, there is hardly anything to live from. Naturally we are going backward, and that happens more quickly than we realize. The future looks rather bleak for us farmers but we hope God will spare us from plague this year, especially the grasshoppers that devour everything—we have not found any of their eggs so maybe there will not be any hatching out.

I see by the papers you have had a hard winter over there. Here it was as usual, with January and February quite cold but very nice since. Should someone from there be emigrating this spring, I hope you might send with them some wool things for me, such as wadmal [coarse, thick wool] and stockings. What I brought with me is long ago worn to shreds and the stuff we get here is not made to last. Many are also asking for wool cards [for cleaning wool].

Nothing further to say regarding myself or family so I will close wishing you the very best for time and for Eternity.

Your
Big Ola[70]

For children old enough to appreciate their surroundings, moving with their parents onto the fenceless prairie—with its endless sweeps of wildflowers, snakes, primitive sod houses, and populations of American Indians—was an unforgettable experience. In spite of her young age, this girl from Michigan, who settled in Dakota Territory with her family, keenly recognized the rapidly evolving nature of the prairie around her family's homestead. What was once the treeless domain of Indians and animals like the buffalo had become home to grazing cattle, plowed fields, new houses, improved roads, and even trees.

Chamberlain, Dak
May 20th 1884
My dear Cousin Barbara,

As it is raining tonight I will try to write a few lines in answer to your welcome letter. This leaves us well. Am sorry about Christina losing her girl. This is the first rain we have had for over one week. Our garden is growing nicely. Corn and potatoes are up and cucumbers, flower seeds are coming up. There are very nice wild flowers out here. Well, Barbara, we had our dance. There were thirty five numbers. Danced three sets all night. We will move into the house next week. I believe I will quit for tonight. My hands are so nervous I make fifty mistakes a minute, so farewell until to-morrow.

Wednesday evening, well Barbara, it rained steady all last night and by the looks of the ground you couldn't tell whether there was a rain or not. I washed yesterday and also today. Am going to Dan's tomorrow if it is a nice day. The mosquitoes are awfully bad. They are large. We are going to have doors and then we won't be troubled. Dan brought us the cutest dog. It is just tearing around with our shoes. I am sorry to hear that Sadie is troubled with a cough. How is Martha, is she still in Monroe? Peter got a letter from Bert. He says Mathies is living on the air, I think it would be mighty poor living.

I wish I was there to go to church with you. There is none near here. We heard a steamboat this morning. That is, they all heard it, with the exception of Peter and I. There were two Indians here Sunday. There was no one at home but mother and I. They wanted to buy some little pigs about a week old. We would not let them have any. I am learning to talk Indian. It seems a great deal easier than any other language. I can count to ninety nine. We had two messes of fresh fish. Am going fishing some Sunday. Oh my, the snakes that have been killed lately. They have just begun to come out. I saw a rattle snake, the first one I ever saw. There are lots of blue racers and bull snakes here. Mike killed two today with his boot. Peter has about forty acres broken and have quite a bit planted. Butter is twenty five cents here now. I am killing mosquitoes by handfulls. We don't have to watch our cows. They eat around the house and maybe they will go about half a mile away and then come home again. Dan has two little ponys. They look cute.

The wildflowers are very pretty. There are three kinds out in the yard. We are going to have a large yard. It is level and in the fall we will plant trees, have a windbreak. I got a dollar for cleaning house after the dance, have not cleaned it yet though. Our buttry is ceiled all through and the cellar door opens into the buttry. Mother sends her love to all. She says tell Aunt Betsy those peaches were good on the road. The roads are splendid now. I have almost forgotten how mud looks. Has Alvin and Ren had the measles? Tell them they are too good or bad, I don't know which. Well, I will close for this time. Answer soon. Give my love to everybody you see,

Your cousin, May [Shrake]

Mother says to tell Alvin she has that rooster feather yet and is going to keep it until she sees him.[71]

LIVING ON AN ISOLATED LAND CLAIM far away from friends, family, and the conveniences of a settled region could be a challenge for children and adults alike. The children of the McCarthy family in Wyoming worried they were so isolated that even Santa Claus would overlook them. Fortunately, the generosity of far-away friends helped to make their Christmas special.

Dear friend, Am in Worland at grocery. Am in a hurry to start home. So cold. Rec'd your box & card. Will write soon. This is a poor little letter for Xmas.
Worland, Wyo.
Dec. 27 [1909?]
Dear friends:

We were so pleased with our Xmas box! Toys were very scarce and very expensive here. I did not feel that I could get any. I filled the stockings with candy and nuts, and John and I sat up till 12 o'clock after children had gone to bed to bake cookies and pull taffy. The children were somewhat

Teachers and students outside a substantial sod schoolhouse in Custer County, Nebraska, about 1888

doubtful as to whether Santa Claus could find them, as they had not told him where they were now located. They discussed the matter very much. I didn't help them any, in fact, discouraged them all I could.

Sat. morning when they came down and found their stockings full of sweets, we opened your box, and I wish you could have seen them. They jumped up and down, and hugged their gifts, and had such a good time all day. Mary paints, Ethel draws and draws, and when she becomes tired of those pictures I slip a postcard under, and it is all new. Grandma says her doiley "is a beauty." She has it in her room. I have long wanted a burnt wood piece, and am so glad to have one of your own work.

I always loved to be remembered, but since I have been out here so far away from all dear friends, and at times just a little bit lonely, I appreciate being remembered a thousands times more than ever in my life. Today (Mon.) John went to Worland, got the rest of our Xmas mail. Such pretty cards from Mrs. Trump. My twin cousin in N.Y. sent the Women's Home Companion a year. The children so pleased with cards from Mrs. Zents and schoolmates. Was so glad she sent one to Mary for she had not received one card or letter since we came here. Occasionally, Paul and Helen receive cards and letters from little people in D.C. Mary is always expecting one, and asking, when the mail comes, "Is one for me?" and today one came. Wish Mrs. Zents could have seen her eyes. These little things mean so much to us all. I really do not feel like writing tonight. Am not in the mood.

Good night,

C. McCarthy

Many thanks from us all for your kindness, and it was so thotful to send it so far ahead of Xmas so that we could have it that morning. They all say they are going to write to Auntie Taylor.[72]

As soon as an area became settled, schools such as the one this young girl attended were often built communally of the same material used for houses, sod in this case. By one count, during the 1870s one school per day was being built in Nebraska to meet the demand for children's education. Small salaries and free land claims were often used to entice teachers— both men and women.[73]

Quinter Kans Gove County—At home
Sunday April 24th 1887
Dear Rhoda & Lucy Sadie & Nettie

Rhoda, I will write a few lines this after noon. Pa got your letter last Wednesday and forgot to give it to us untill today. I was glad to hear from you. Is Nettie well again? I and Maggie are going to school; our school commensed two weeks ago tomorrow. I like my teacher real well. Her

Name is Miss Cora Evans. What is your teachers name? I study fifth reader, Arithmetic, Spelling & Geography & History. What do you and Lucy study & does Len go up stairs to school yet? We go to school in a sod schoolhouse. It is just the size of our house. There are eleven scholars coming to school. We have one mile and a half to walk. Does Sadie & Nettie & Lucy have big times? I get awfull lonesome without them. Tell Grandma that Maggie never had a dress to fit her better than the one you

A rural school with teacher, 12 students, and three horses for transportation

sent with Henrys things. Well I cant think of any more this time. Kiss the babbies, love to all,

write soon.

Yours Truly

S. E. Oblinger

P.S. Maggie & I stayd alone one week & stayed alone nights to and pa is going out to Gove City tomorrow and we will be alone this week.[74]

Clowning around with masks at the Brenna homestead, probably Minnesota, 1915

7

Socializing and Adventuring

It is not surprising that settlers living on the open prairie frequently desired interactions with one another, a tradition that continues today. The same determined spirit that produced homes of sod and fields of grain collectively built churches, schools, and meeting halls. Farmers and ranchers organized farm and prairie populist movements as a way of unifying against economic and governmental forces that seemed to work against them. Local social organizations, including ethnic ladies aid societies, were created to help those in need.

In addition to the creation of social, political, and governmental networks, settlers found other ways to intermingle. They traveled for hours to spend the night with friends. They turned the cramped quarters of a homestead or barn into the site of a party, where they listened to music, danced, and held dinners that sometimes lasted until the early morning hours. Traveling ministers offered religious services in private homes. Settlers celebrated holidays such as the Fourth of July with vigor, and political speeches were widely attended. Families ventured together across the prairie, journeying by horseback to rivers, to remote places with trees, and, in late summer, to their favorite berry-harvesting locations. They hunted game for sport and food.

A woman who had spent several years on the North Dakota prairie before her family moved to escape the "bracing climate" of the region wrote about this desire for human contact in a remembrance in 1962. She noted that her "folks never turned anyone away," always welcoming strangers and friends alike into their home. "If they could eat what we had, they could stay."[75]

The legacy of the efforts of settlers to seek out and create opportunities to socialize with one another still exists. Ethnic heritage celebrations like Nebraska's Danish Grundlovs Fest, South Dakota's Czech Days, and North Dakota's Ukrainian Festival occur every year throughout the Great Plains. Rodeos and county and state fairs are widely attended, as are Sweet Corn Days in Iowa and Prairie Fest in Montana. Parades and potluck picnics celebrating holidays, graduations, and community events fill small-town parks throughout the summer.

*SETTLERS USED ALMOST ANY OPPORTUNITY to get together
for celebrations and picnics, including patriotic Fourth of July
festivals like the one the author describes to his sister. Ironically, although the attendees at this event were celebrating the
existence of the nation, the first Americans were only invited to
the table for the leftovers. At the time, American Indians had no
legal citizenship in the land where their ancestors had lived
long before Europeans arrived, so the oath of allegiance Robert
mentions would not have been administered to them. Citizenship for Native Americans waited until 1924.*[76]

Salina [Kansas] July 7th 1861

Dear Sister

I expect you have been thinking that I have forgoton you altogether saying I never have wrote you a letter since I left home. But such is not the
case for I often think of you and wonder how you are getting along in the
new conditions of life into which you entered but a few days before I left
home. I hope you are striving to making a good wife to Mr Anderson.
I have wrote three letters to father and Mother since I come here and as yet
have not received a scrape of a favor from either of them. I have been looking for a letter from home every time the mail come in for the last month
but I looked in vain, I have given up the idea of getting a letter from them,
I now look to you for home news. I hope you wont disapoint me to, Write
as soon as you receive this and tell me how you are all getting along in
these troublous times, and if any of the young men in Flat Prairie have
enlisted in to the united States service, and who they are.

We had a grand union celebration here on the fourth of July. The
program was first, the reading of the declaration of independence, next the
administering of the oath of allegiance to the government to all present,
both men and women. Next was an oration by Colenol Philips on the State
of the country and the duty of all loyal citizens; it was the best oration
I ever heard. Next was a free dinner got up by the ladies of Salina and
neighbourhoods; it was equal to any public dinner I ever saw got up, thére
was every thing there that the heart of man could desire. After all the set-
telers had partaken we invited to the table over thirty Indians who had
been looking on all the time we were eating. They were mostly [women
and children]. It was the laughiblest farce I ever seen. Some sitting some
standing and some of them half lying on the table but all seemly strieving
who could fill their wames [stomachs] with the one hand and their wallets
with the other fastest. After they got through eating we gathered up what
was left and gave it to them to take home. When they started off they
looked as if they thought a union celebration a good thing. Their camp is
about a mile and a half out of town; there is always some of them in town

every day. They bring in wild goosberrys and curens that they get growing on the hills and sells them to the folks in town. They are good to eat when cooked; the goosberrys is rather small but the curans is equal in size to any I ever saw cultivated in gardens. Mother and you used to speculate and talk about how foolish it was for young folks to go to Kansas and suffer the privations that you imagined, for they were all imaginery privations they had to suffer. I for my part has had as good victuals to eat and as good a bed to ly in as I ever had at home, and every other lady that I know of is doing well enough. James intends moving down to his claim this week. His house is not quite finished but it will do to live in to fall well enough. He dug a well and got plenty of good water. It will sute both him and Willie better than living in town; they will both be close to there work.

Willie wished me to write you to tell father that the plow he wants him to send out is a ten inch two horse plow. Tom Anderson is out hunting Bufalo at present; he intends hunting all summer if he can make it pay. Him and I intends putting in some wheat this fall on James claim. Robert Crawford is breaking the land for us. We would have put it in on our own claims had we been able to fence it. I am still working for Mr Philips at his sawmill. I dont think I will come home this fall; I believe it will be better for me to stay here and put some fencing on my claim while there is a chance of getting timber off public land.

I was down with Willie and James this morning to see there corn. It is looking uncommon well; if the season holds on as favorable it will give a large yield. We are all well at present. I hope this will find you all enjoying the same blessing. Give my best to your brother

Robert Muir[77]

American Indians visit a fenced homestead in western South Dakota to ask for water.

MRS. E. E. "LULU" BENJAMIN recounts for her friend—Mary Esther Vilas of Madison, Wisconsin—coming face-to-face with a bear while on a three-week wood-gathering adventure with her neighbors. The lack of prairie trees caused many settlers to travel great distances to find wood suitable for fences and fuel. In spite of the close call with the bear and the fact that she lived alone on the Montana prairie—her nearest neighbor was six miles away—she said she felt perfectly safe and never saw the need to learn how to use a gun.

A single parent, Benjamin traveled from Iowa to Montana in the mid-1890s to homestead, one of many single mothers who staked out their own claims. Under the Homestead Act, a married woman could not file for land in her own name unless she could prove that she was the head of the household. In spite of the difficulties associated with living on the plains, Lulu not only made a home for her son but also served as a foster mother for a succession of orphaned girls. Mary Vilas, a frequent correspondent, often sent clothing and other household items to help make her life in Montana easier.

[1920]

My Dear Mrs Vilas

Perhaps it will be a passing interest to you for me to write some of my adventures homesteading in Montana. Our land lays near the borders of Montana, Wyoming & So Dakota—our homesteads lay in a flat valley—no trees no brush except a few here & there on streams or water holes. 25 miles from our place on the Wyoming side in the hills, or Sheep mountains, as they are called, is where we go to get our wood. We call this place "The Pines." The hills are thickly covered with wonderful pine trees—this section is all government land and the settlers are allowed to cut the dead or dying timbers & haul the pine cones for their supply of fuel. It is the custom of settlers to club together two & three families & go in the fall while the good weather is on & camp for 3 or 4 weeks at a time & cut their wood & fence posts for the years supply & then haul it home. The cutting is all done before the hauling home is commenced & the big long trees hauled by 4 to 6 horses is a great sight. Each man has his own supply marked out & no one bothers his outfit no matter how long a time elapses before his hauling is finished—should any man be found meddling with another man's property—he would be found hanging to a tree, consequently we have no pilfering in this country.

The first trip we made to the Pines we joined a party of twelve—I drove my own team, rode in my buggy with my son then too small to handle an ax—I had hired a neighbor man to drive my other team & wagon for hauling, he was to do my felling of [trees]. I can never forget my feeling of awe on that first entrance I made to the Pines—we all took tents, bedding, cooking utensils & food—we located where there was a cute log cabin so I was domiciled there and agreed to do the cooking for the crowd—my son & three other women were to gather cones while the men chopped down trees—they would be far from the camp & all took guns not only for protection but in case of wild game. The men explained to me I must learn to use a gun for my own protection but I thot a signal from the big dinner bell would bring me the help I needed if danger came—

The men hung the big bell & left me alone in the camp early next morning. I had brot a straw tick filled with straw for my bed as I knew I could not sleep on the ground. The hut had an opening front and back— the men had set up our camp stove—put up shelves for our food & dishes & improvised a pretty good dinning room table—I remember how busy I was & how my mind was dwelling that morning on my dear parents & was wondering if they would not raise in their graves if they knew what I was up against—no fear was in my heart. Just then I heard the rustling of leaves & looking out the back door I saw a big reddish brown bear swaggering along toward my back door his head down close to the ground wagging his head making a howling noise—there was the shot gun hanging on the wall but I did not know the first thing about handling a gun— I guess I dident even think of that, I just skipped out the front door, pulled the bell rope & ran yelling toward the place where I knew the men were— the men said afterward the only thing that kept the bear from chasing me was the smell of the fresh meat I had cooking & that was what he was scenting with his head down—the men came running with their guns on hearing my screams of help—help—bear—bear—as they passed me I said "in the hut" & sure enough he was in the hut when they got there with his nose in my straw tick, rooting out the straw & bedding torn up. It dident take but a minute for three shots to come firing at him. He stretched out with an angry growl & was soon dead. He had pulled the kettle of beef off the stove but on account of being hot could not eat it, he then pulled a gallon can of syrup off the shelve & chewed it in two & what he did not lap up was on the floor. Evidently his next move was to scent the fresh straw in my bed—all this was done in much less time than it takes me to write it—when I got back to the house the animal was dead. I was in a state of utter collapse. The men took the bear out, strung him on poles head down— skinned him—cut him up as they would a steer & we cooked and ate every atom of the meat. It was fine. Did you ever taste young bear meat? If not you dont know what you have missed.

All this was a great wonderment to my boy and he tells this story much better than I for he tells how my long black hair (now white) was streaming over my face & how I lost my house shoe & cut a deep gash on my foot

& how he cried at the sight of the blood gushing from my foot thinking I had shot myself. Wasent it funny I did not attempt to handle the gun. John puts a funny touch to the story telling how he felt when he first tasted bear meat. We still have that bear skin. The men said at that time no bear had been seen in that section for a long time & none since. They expected the mate would follow up but he did not.

We were in this camp 3 weeks but I was not left there alone—the other women could handle a gun as well as the men so one of them always stayed with me. In all these years I have not learned to handle a gun. Tonight I am alone—6 miles to the nearest neighbor. I look at the two big guns hanging on the side wall and if danger came I would be helpless—I never fear man—we have no bad men in this country & few wild animals. Some fine conditions, for no bad women either.

Now & then a bad woman shows up out here & as soon as she is known to be a bad woman a delegation of good men & women wait upon her and give her certain length of time to leave the country and if she does not go, then the men of this delegation go after her, put her in a lumber wagon & take her to Miles [City] & turn her over to the officers. This has only happened a few times in the years I have lived here. The sharpest thorn I have had in this country is the association with ignorance. I have learned to rise above all the inharmonous temperments except dense ignorance. Since you & your precious daughter have come into my life, many of the hard spots here have been softened—I always think of your lives being full of wonderful possibilities & that you have both been a power of goodness in the world. In my daily prayers I do not forget you & your goodness to me in all my efforts that brings much joy to my quiet ranch life. With best wishes and much gratitude.

Yours Very Truly

Mrs E. E. Benjamin

Sept 17–20[78]

IN ADDITION TO THE LEVEL, FERTILE LAND, *this settler cites the vast amount of wild game as one of the benefits of living on the prairie. When the first non-Indian settlers appeared on the Great Plains, the region was teeming with wildlife, and many families supplemented their diets and income with rabbits, antelope, deer, bison, prairie chickens, wild turkeys, and fur-bearing animals such as coyotes. Not surprisingly, as plowed fields replaced the prairie, wildlife quickly disappeared, especially bison, which, the author notes, "leave as fast as the country gets settled up." Once numbering in the tens of millions, bison—sometimes referred to as buffalo—were hunted en masse by the likes of Buffalo Bill Cody to feed hungry railroad construction crews. Later, commercial hunters slaughtered them by the millions to meet the demand for buffalo hide coats. By 1890, less than twenty years after this letter was written, it was believed that only 1,000 bison remained. Today, due largely to the efforts of the American Bison Society and others, there are an estimated 150,000 to 200,000 bison on private and public reserves throughout the United States.[79]*

Verona, Hamilton Co, Nebraska, Dec 20th 1871
Dr. A A Rowley
Dear Sir,

I write you at this time to inform you that I am still in the land of the living and myself and family are all well as usual. Hoping you and yours and Mother and her family are enjoying the same blessings. I should have wrote you before this time but thought I should wait until I could give you some history of this new country.

I am at present living on the farm of a Mitchell Moore in Hamilton Co but shall settle in Clay County, the next county south of this. I have taken 160 acres of the finest Prairie that I ever set my eyes upon. It is as level as that of Jon Leffles on Nine Mound Prairie and is just ½ mile from the depot on the Burlington and Missouri rail road. Said rail road is a new road just about completed. It is all graded through to Fort Karney on the Platt river where it intersects the Union Pacific road for California. The track is all laid to the west line of Clay Co. and the cars running to that place. The depot I have reference to is on the west county line of Clay Co. and is not named yet. Consequently I cant give you the name of it. There are only four houses built there as yet, but as soon as spring opens there will be a general rush on the line of this road and the land will all be picked up for miles on each side of it. Those wishing to settle along these rail roads must be here in time or they must fall back to the rear. You can form no idea how fast this country is settling up. There were some twenty thousand families crossed the Missouri river at Platts Mouth this last fall besides those that are at other points. I expect these 20 thousand were only a drop in the bucket compared to other places.

I will now give a brief discription of this country as far as I have seen it. Timber is rather limited. There is none; only what you find imediately on the streams and that consists only of Elm, Boxelder, Ash, and Honey locust and rather scrubby at that. But after you leave the streams from one to two miles on what they call the first raise, here you come on the Prairie and such country you never set your eyes upon just as far as the eye can see there is one vast plain of prairie just as level as a floor and the soil ranges from two to six or more feet deep of the richest quality, a black loam which will produce all kind of crops that man can think of—all kinds of fruit will grow here in abundance without any trouble. All it wants is the planting. It is just the country for me. Let others do as they please but give me this country.

It is true we have a savere winter here this winter but this does not discourage me as the oldest settlers tells me that such a winter they never saw here for fifteen years. It set in cold on the 22nd day of November and froze up and the ground has been covered with snow ever since and some days it is very cold. We have a good log house here and plenty of wood so we will be all right on the goose. We keep four cows and five horses and plenty to keep them till spring. Theodore & Charlott are living on the next farm adjoining George Rhinehart and Warren P White & families & John Proud are all here from Verona together with any number of the Scotch boys from the Sugar river, all old acquaintance so that I am well satisfied and do not get the blues.

Jacob Zink & John H Shuman & Delan Moore are out on the plains since the 25th day of Nov killing Buffaolo, Elk, Deer, Wolves, Wild Cats, and are trapping for furrs. They have sent in a load of meet and furrs & wild turkey and expect to stay out until about the first of March when they will start for home. When they come home you will see John and he will give you a full history of his campaign. I expect they just enjoy the sport. I should have been with them but when I got here I had to put up stables and shelter for my stock so that I could not get ready in time but if I live until next year I shall kill a Buffalo. I expect without fail there are a great many out fits here going to the plains after buffalo every winter. They must go some 5 miles west of here now as the buffalo leave as fast as the country gets settled up but the country about here are full of Antelope through the summer. There are some deer and turkeys here as yet and thousands of Prairie chicks + grouse and rabits by the thousands, also plenty of Jack rabits. These are as large as my dog Seymore. There are also what they call Swifts [coyotes]. They are a species of wolf, kind of between a wolf & fox and have very fine furr. John Felick caught four of them, two coons, two mink, and one Beaver for which furs he got $4.50, and he sold too soon as he should have got more for them.

It is getting mail time therefor I must quit writing at this time by giving you all our best respects and each of you a merry christmas from your old friend and well wishes.

Joseph Flick

Send me a paper if you can[80]

A DAUGHTER AND HER MOTHER wrote the following letters to relatives left behind in Monroe, Wisconsin, when they settled in Dakota Territory. In spite of the cold weather, holidays like Christmas and New Year's were treasured as opportunities for families and neighbors to gather to socialize and share with each other the bounties of their farms. They also provided

settlers with the chance to partake in one of their favorite so-
cial activities—dances. Held in a barn, a house, or a dance
hall in town, dances were often accompanied by a fiddle player
or just a mouth harp. Dances were popular among nearly all
social classes. Many ethnic enclaves brought their own style of
dance with them, including the Polish polka and the German
schottische.

Chamberlain (Dakota Territory)
Jan 18th 1885
My Dear Cousin Barbara,

I received your letter a few weeks ago. It found us all well and leaves us all with bad colds, but we are improving. The weather has been quite cold here this winter. The old residents say, 'tis the coldest, for nineteen years but I know I have seen colder in Wis. I don't get scared any. I know it will soon be spring. One good thing we don't have any mud to wade about in.

You may be sure I remember Reub Garrisons dance. Was not that a fearful cold time. I shiver now with the thoughts of that cold, cold room Maggie and I used to sleep in, wasn't it awful. I have a nice warm room now. The stove pipe goes through and there is a fire day and night. How nice it is.

Peter and Mike have gone to Lafe's to spend the evening. They wanted me to go but I thought I was better off at home, so here I am. Christmas day we all went to Lafe's for a turkey roast, we were going to a dance that night, but the wind blew and blew & blew, so we stayed at home. New Year's we had a dinner and we went to a dance. Oh my, wasn't it cold. I had to tie a scarf around my head while I was dancing. There was a dance last Friday, but we did not go. There will be one next Fri, if our colds are better we may attend. . . .

I went to see my [claim?] shanty the other day. Snow had blown in some. Mike is thinking of taking a claim, but is not sure yet. I will close for this time, hoping to hear from you soon, I remain your affectionate Cousin, My love to all.

Was you churning when Uncle Reub came? Lafe has the rheumatism now. He is not able to do very much. Mother says she thinks of you every time she smashes potatoes. (The reason is that you are about as soft as they are, ha ha ha ha ha, he he he he he, ho ho ho ho)

My Dear Sister & Brother,

Good evening, how do you do, one and all. We had a turkey Christmas at Lafe's. Hope you had one too. We had chickens New Years, why did you not come and help eat them. I have had a very bad cold this last week, but am getting better. We had a peck of apples for Christmas, they are two dollars per bu. Butter is twenty five cts, eggs 25 cts. I am sorry you are not

Feasting and festivities at what is probably a barn-warming party on the Joe Pazandak farm, 1910s

feeling well but hope you are better, and still continue so. I wish I could have tasted your pies, I bet they were good. We butchered two hogs on the Monday before New Years, made sausages, liverworst, mince meat. Made some mince pies yesterday. What has ever become of Bate. Do you ever see him. We have not heard of him since we left there. Do you ever hear from Sister Mille and the rest.

Please write soon,

Your Sister Katie

I look at your picture every day. Give our love to Mahala. I am sorry she is not feeling well.[81]

Settlers frequently attended dinners and parties at each other's homes, sometimes traveling for hours to get there. Usually, the hosts would use the occasion as an opportunity to show off their finest china and silver, even if their home was a dugout. In this letter, an impudent young woman homesteading with her family in North Dakota tells her friend in Wisconsin that life in a claim shack on the prairie does not lack for style or entertainment. She makes a number of racial affronts aimed at American Indians, African Americans, and ethnic Germans from Russia who, at the time, were arriving by the tens of thousands in North Dakota.

[July 31, 1907]

[Leipzig, North Dakota]

Dear Helen:

Suppose you girls are saying "Poor Bess" and feeling dreadfully sorry for me out here in the wild and wooly uncivilized regions of America. But really time just seems to fly. I haven't done half I had planned and I am afraid winter will be here before we are ready for it. I've sewed some, done a little fancy work and lots of darning and mending but most of my time has been spent out of doors digging in the garden and riding.

I look just like the Russian inhabitants for I am as black as a squaw. The sun out here fairly bakes one and it is such a bother to always run for a sunbonnet and "kid" gloves. I declare I dont believe any Viroqua people would care to recognize me for I do show there is no shade about here.

Oh! but I do dress in style. Mother brought out all the old duds from the attic and this is a grand place to save your clothes and wear out old timers. You can see a team miles away. Up one valley we can see ten miles (up the Cannon Ball river)—so when any one starts to our shack, if we see them in time we can comb our hair, change our gowns and get a good meal in running order before they arrive. You see Dakota has some redeeming qualities.

Wish you could come out, but I suppose you think I am too far away. I have the neatest little shack I've seen and "my crops" are tip top. I know you would enjoy our camp life for a short time.

I have a new bronco. He is white and has two brands (Y.H. and S.P.) on him. He was surely a bucking bronco when we got him but now he is real dignified, except at times, then he lays back his ears, flips his head on one side and you have to dig in your heels and knees and hold on for dear life. However I think he will become civilized in due time by merely associating with me—ha! ha! Riding horseback in Viroqua isn't in it at all. Here you dont have to be bothered with fences and roads but just go any old way you wish. Twelve miles when you mail or get a letter isn't any ride at all. I rode 20 mi. last Saturday and 20 Sunday and I try at least 10 every day.

Jess Cobb is here—he has filed on a claim that is only a couple of miles from here and will stay with us till it is time to live there. Tell you it is nice to have him here for he is so good to help papa, not to say anything about having company. You get so sick of seeing Russians and hearing them spiel Dutch. You ask them anything and its always "ich nicht fur stehe [verstehe]" and they shrug their shoulders and look idiotic. Sometimes you fool them and try to ramble off a little Dutch and then they can't do enough for you. Ah! we don't live in the United States any more for this is "Little Russia."

A party at Mrs. Olson's Montana claim shack draws neighbors from miles around.

Say, do you remember the Herrons, who used to live near Viroqua? Well you know they live twenty miles north of here on a claim and I was up there a week ago. (Mr. Herron is Mrs. Rayner's brother and Mrs. Herron is the Horton girl who adopted Nellie Mutch's baby—now do you know them?)

I went up to stay a few days, when the children went back from visiting here, but I had such a fine time that my stay lengthened into two weeks. I felt rather strange in a real house but I survived and tried not to be too green.

There is a settlement of young people from Kentucky about six miles west of Mr. Herron's and they are surely a jolly bunch. There is a Fannie Grey and her brother, who live in a dug-out in the side of a small hill. They are fine. We were there to a supper one night and the whole crowd was to dinner one afternoon. You can tell they are used to things for the table was set up fine with good silver and nice china. Fannie is a good cook although she never did any till she came out here and that was sometime in May. She always had a coon to do her cooking, washing, etc. They are building them a nice little cottage now so the days of their sod shack are numbered.

Fannie was at Herrons the first week I was there and on Sunday Mrs. Herron invited the five Kentucky boys over, besides the folks were there and a Russian family by the name of Lempke. (23 in all.)—not all Lempke's though. I was to go home that Sun. with the folks but times were too good so I stayed.

The next week we picniced on the Cannon Ball, went to a swell supper and a dance at the sheep-camp-ranch (in my honor) and I had to tear myself away on Saturday—missing a dance—ten miles west—just because I had stayed so long.

Well I hope Viroqua is as lively as we are out here. . . . don't forget to write soon.

Lovingly,

Bess [Cobb][82]

In spite of her family's and neighbors' struggles with ongoing drought and economic uncertainty, life continued to move forward for this young woman and her friends in North Dakota. In a letter to her friend living in Canada, she describes her adventures berry picking, attending dances, school socials, birthday parties, and Ladies Aid Society sales, and watching a new town spring up from the prairie.

Frettim, No. Dak.

7-20-1911

My dear friend:

Your Honest Albert, are you really sore at me or no doubt you've been detained as I sometimes am. But I've not heard from you for so long, almost thinking you've forgotten me. Well the crops and every thing are in need of rain here, and are dying for want of it. So I guess the ones that remain here will see starvation before another harvest if drought keeps up. How is everything up there? I have the impression pa will come there this fall. He is thinking of renting some of his horses out and take some with him. He has wrote to Kenyon Minn. where his folks are to find out how the crops are there, also the sale for horses, and as soon as he hears from there he will know more what to do. He was thinking of shipping a carload there providing the chances were good.

I was just about to ask you how you spent the 4th but they don't celebrate there do they? I had an exceptionally good time. I went home with our teacher and staid a week during the 4th. Was up nine nights in succesion. Now don't say I'm bad. ha. ha.

The Friday before the 4th I went to a school entertainment & the next night we had ours & a basket social [potluck] with it. . . . I was at Ladies Aid sales and birthday parties. So after I got home I didn't do much else only sleep. I know I was crazy but I wasn't the only one. My chum, the teacher, was in it too. Bessie, Wilber, Tot & Carrie all celebrated the same place I did. Don't know what kind of a time they had.

A few weeks ago pa moved the windmill out in the pasture & now the days are so hot & still that the mill won't move so we have to drive the horses to the lake just the same. I just came back from one of the trips now.

New towns on the northern Great Plains such as Lemmon, South Dakota, became social centers for homesteaders and other settlers.

They are alright on cool days but believe me when it comes to 105 in the shade. . . .

Spect I told you of papa being at the hospital a couple of times. He just got back last night from there but he only went for more medicine then. But he was there before the fourth and staid nearly a month. He has rhuematism of the heart so bad. They treated him by giving him baths but it didn't seem to do much good. Tho he has quite a few different kinds of medicine.

Last Wednesday a girl friend & I went to pick June berries; we only got about 4 quarts but I lost my glasses in the deal which was worth more than all the berries. So I was to Steele yesterday and expect I'll get them next mail day.

Well the new town of Robinson contains old Shaws Store is about all besides a post office and pool room and blacksmith shop. But they think it's the only town on the continent. They celebrated there and have had quite a few dances but I never went to more than one & that was the first, and I don't plan on attending any more there either so there. ha. ha. Well I guess I must ring off as it is nearly dinner time and suppose this means for me to get to work.

Now write soon and don't wait as long as I did. And I will never, never, never, neglect again.

I remain as ever

Your Friend, Elma [Frettim][83]

A girl fills a barrel with water from a spring at LeRoy, Montana, 1913.

8

Fire and Ice

The harsh prairie environment created serious challenges for settlers who first lived in sod houses and poorly built claim shacks. Many families had never experienced flesh-freezing windchills, droughts, or violent storms. Many were ill equipped physically and emotionally to deal with the physical confrontations of the region.

Surprised settlers faced the droughts of the "Great American Desert"—droughts that sucked the life out of crops and dried up vital surface water. Sometimes the droughts lasted for years, even stunting the native prairie grass. On the semiarid western reaches of the plains, drought or no drought, rainfall levels were constantly inadequate for raising most crops.

Inhabitants also had to contend with the wind. Whether blowing gently or hard enough to tear buttons off one's shirt, it never seemed to stop—spring, summer, fall, or winter. Its constant roar drove some settlers mad. Drought and wind fed prairie fires begun by lightning strikes and careless settlers. Dry lightning—lightning without rain—was a phenomenon common to the region. Fires frequently burned tens of thousands of acres of prairie and anything else standing in their way. Moving swiftly, they were capable of running down humans and animals alike.

Then there were blizzards and tornadoes—both of which have to be experienced to be truly understood. Tornadoes could strike with little or no warning and destroy years of hard work in seconds, killing livestock, flattening crops, and lifting houses into the air and smashing them to pieces. (It wasn't by chance that Kansas was the setting for the Wizard of Oz stories—the author had lived on the Great Plains.) Blizzards and ground blizzards (fallen snow picked up and driven horizontally by high winds) could quickly freeze settlers and livestock to death.

This troublesome Great Plains climate has made the people living there resilient, innovative, and constantly prepared for sudden and dangerous changes in the weather. The plains is home to "tornado alley," which stretches from north Texas to North Dakota and is marked by frequent life-threatening tornadoes. It was the location of the 1930s Dustbowl and the Great Flood of 1993, the most expensive flood in U.S. history, which claimed fifty lives and caused $15 billion in damages. A blizzard in eastern Colorado in 1997 produced snowdrifts as high as fifteen feet and took the lives of five stranded motorists. A year later, a blizzard in Nebraska, Kansas, and Iowa blew furiously for more than a day, dumping snow and dropping windchills to nearly fifty degrees below zero. The phrase "If you don't like the weather, wait a minute" is commonly heard in almost every state of the Great Plains.[84]

In this letter a settler describes for her father one of the Great Plains' most memorable attributes—the wind. The average wind velocity in Nebraska, where the writer lived, is ten miles per hour, but some locations in the state average almost seventeen miles per hour. When wind blows over freshly plowed fields, dust and dirt blow everywhere. Soil erosion, which occurs when wind velocity reaches twelve miles per hour one foot above the surface of the ground, continues to be a serious problem affecting nearly the entire Great Plains.[85]

Camp Creek [Nebraska] Mar. 30 1880
Dear Papa:

You may think you have blows East, but I can tell you, you can't hold a candle to the west. It is blowing hard today but nothing to what it did Saturday. The people around here say they have seen nothing like it for years. I don't know at what rate the wind blew but I'm pretty sure greased lightning could not begin to keep up. The dust was so thick that we couldn't see anything. You could hardly stand on your feet out doors. Most of the farm buildings are roofed with hay or straw and a number of haystacks are around in the yards. They had to put boards and logs on them to keep them from blowing away, and that did not prevent some of the hay from blowing away. People kept in the house mostly. Will went over to the other farm to work in the morning but did not do anything, instead he went off with one of the boys shooting ducks. They did not get any however and Will came home with the Blackest & dirtiest face I ever saw on any one. not even the "Gormanite."

The next morning you would never have thought there had been a blow the day before. Just as lovely on Easter as you ever saw. Phil and John and I went up to the City to an Episcopal church and had the excruciating pleasure of having Prof. Simons sing a solo and flatting terribly. He passed me without looking at me.

We will try and get your dirt for you. I shall get some on the West farm, that is Aunt Sarah's. You can get enough any where, even on the windowsills.

You ask about the hills. There are hills near the river but as you go back in the country ten miles you find level prairie. The hills some of them are as high as Capt. Burr's but most of them are rounded like the home lot.

The boys just brought a great hen hawk right up in our room to show mamma and I. It was simply immense. We are going to try and save one of the wings to take home.

This morning Will shot the handsomest duck I ever saw. It is a wood duck and builds its nest in trees. We think of sending it to you to get stuffed. There is not one around this country that knows anything about stuffing birds. It will be a nice thing to have a Nebraska duck and a handsome one. There are very few to be found I hear.

I have my hands full taking care of three young rabbits—between the cats & dogs I don't know as I shall be able to raise them. They are cunning [cute] I can tell you most all ears and they snuggle up together as cunning as can be. John makes them drink their milk I tell you. The boys are all real kindhearted.

Wed morn. We have just packed the duck. I hope it will go all right. We wet some of the cotton in cloxallum so as to keep it. If it don't cost too much, get it stuffed. Mamma says don't spend too much. I don't think she would mind four or five dollars. Any way you can see a Nebraska bird. If it costs too much to send it we may keep it to eat.

Give my love to all inquiring friends.

[Eugenie Hathaway][86]

WITH HER HUSBAND IN TOWN, letter writer Martha Janney describes being alone and stranded inside a poorly constructed claim shack during a blizzard. To survive, she retreats to the root cellar and records two terror-filled days in her journal. The snow is so heavy and blowing so fiercely that she cannot leave the shack to feed the animals for fear of getting lost and freezing to death. Root cellars, which were dug beneath houses for the purpose of storing food in the cool ground, served a dual purpose when the weather turned bad.

[West Point, Nebraska]
Monday, November 16 [1868]

The rain ceased about 4 oclock yesterday. A perfect gale set in from the North. I went to shut the Chickens up, and give the Hog her corn, (2 buckets) some siding, short pieces from the pile, had blown off and I went but a short distance for them, but the cold was too intense for my poor fingers, and I got them a little frosted. I put them in cold water, but they have hurt ever since—Last night I went to bed quite comfortable, but slept very little on account of the dreadful storm. I found my bed nearly covered with Snow this morning. The storm continues, wood nearly gone, and I cannot get out for more, neither can I get across the lot, to feed the Hog or Chicks—Poor kitties are in their Cave, and hungry I know—I must resort to the Cellar or perish with cold.

November 17th

After an early supper I came down, brought a Pan of coals, and the Lamp and Candle. Sat and read the blessed word awhile, concluded I could not sit up all night, but tried to get my Big Chair down, but failed brought down Bed and Bedding, sat up and knit untill I was tired then committed my all to the kind care of my Heavenly Father, knowing that he careth for us, and he doeth all things well. Slept but little. The storm continued all night— This morning I went up, made a fire, and put on the Corn and Potatoes for the Hog, got it ready, but Alas, the storm still rages and I cannot venture out. I cannot see the stable, or pig pen, or Coop—Poor things must they all perish? or will the Lord spare them to us? I heard Kitty mewing, but I dare not go out to give her food—I find it is growing colder in the Cellar, quite uncomfortable. Poor, dear, Lewis I know he is uneasy about me—Lord thou knowest all about us. "Thou canst rebuke the storm, Thou canst return him in safety" The poor Emigrants, How they must suffer—Lord send relief, we leave us in thy hands, Thy will be done, Amen

Tuesday Evening in the Cellar.

Gratitude fills my heart—the Lord has rebuked the storm, and the wind is lulled. I found our Hog alive, and very hungry—I fed her, and gave her some hay. Poor kitties are frozen some and their mother is gone—I will let them stay in untill the Snow goes away.

Fighting an advancing prairie fire in New England, North Dakota

November 18th

The storm abated on yesterday about sunset, I got out to feed the stock. Pa came last night, and we slept in the cellar—and this day he has taken out Snow all day long—many, many bushels—Our house is very cold and I cannot work—Nothing can be done now to make it more comfortable. The Lord is our only comfort, in him I trust—he knows all about us.[87]

FIRE IS A NATURAL OCCURRENCE on the prairie and important to its health. Fire burns away old grass and invasive weeds. The combination of wind, grass, and a lack of rainfall made most of the Great Plains region prone to fire, which was potentially deadly for its human and animal residents. Lightning strikes, sparks from trains, a dropped match, or an overturned lantern could result in a prairie fire; some burned for days. When driven by high winds, they could burn a truly remarkable area, as Mrs. Clifford Jencks details to her daughter in this letter. Settlers who didn't live in "fireproof" sod houses often stacked fieldstone or sod around their houses and barns as a precaution to protect them from a prairie fire.

The town where this letter was postmarked—Brushie, South

Dakota—sprang up like many other small towns in response to the early 1900s homesteading boom in western South Dakota. Like the boom, Brushie's existence was short lived; the town disappeared in 1912.

Brushie, S.D.
March 24, 1910
Dear Maybel and all:

Perhaps you may think it strange to receive another letter so soon and written this week when we are so busy getting ready for the doings of the wedding, but I thought you would see by the papers of the disastrous prairie fire which swept over the country. By a low estimate at least 25 miles wide and perhaps a hundred or more miles long. It swept over us and took all our hay and barn. We worked like Turks but to no avail, but the wind was blowing a perfect hurricane. We had fresh breaking north and east of the house and we took the wagon and brought the harness to the house and caught the chickens and put them in the house, all but four which we could not catch and two of those were burned to death and two were scorched so we killed them. Our house is well sodded up on the north and west, the direction from which the fire came. Our claim was entirely burned over, but if we have plenty of rain we may be able to cut all the hay we will need. Edna's claim was burned over all but the house stands as that is where her crop was and protected it. Only burning over about 30 acres of John's claim and he lost nothing. One of our neighbors lost his barn and one horse. George Wallace, formerly of Springfield, lost his barn, hay, corn and some chickens. Our corn was stored here at the house so saved it. Our barn was partly dug out and about four feet above ground of boards and had board roof but probably would not have burned if it had not stood so near the hay stack.

The first of next week Papa will go to the breaks [wooded ravines] for poles and posts and then sod up above the dug out and make a roof of poles and hay and dirt. I tell you sod is the stuff in this country for houses and barns. The fire passes over them and never harms them. We are all well. Edna and I put on overalls and rubber boots to fight fire. You should have seen us. We don't know whether Ellis Williams were burned over or not yet. Papa and I were over there about ten days ago and staid all night, one night. Had a good visit with them. They had a little colt and it was a nice colt. They will be over to the wedding we expect. She will help me, and Papa and Ellis are to wait on table[s] and we will dish up and pour coffee and then we four will eat last. Now don't worry over our little loss for if it rains and sunshines, grass will grow again and make more hay and we will fix up another barn. As long as we keep well we can get along all right. After the affair is over will write as soon as I can. Wish you were here. We are looking for Papa's cousin, Mrs. Gussison and her husband. Well, it is getting late and must close and get up early tomorrow morning and have bread to mix yet—so good night.

Lovingly,
Mamma[88]

DIARY ENTRIES by an unknown author living in western South Dakota detail the scarcity of water during a period of drought. The drought of 1910–11 in that part of the state began an exodus of homesteaders that continued through the 1930s and beyond. In 1910 much of western South Dakota consisted of 160-acre homesteads. Today the average ranch is approximately 5,000 acres.[89]

July 1910

Went to Sorensens to fit dress again and got ½ pail of water—water very scarce. Worked on the Mrs. S's dress—must have it by the 4th; man hollowed "hello" from road, wanted to know if I had any water, said he wanted drink for dog; I rose up, gave dog water; wanted to pay me for it—

Experimental rainmaking machines combating the lack of rainfall in Nebraska

but I said no. Then he thanked me very kindly and gave me 10 bananas, 3 lemons and one orange, quite a handout wasn't it? Half hour later another man drove up and ask for drink—but said no; water a scarce article these times.

Worked on Mrs. S's dress in fore noon; went to town in afternoon; stopped at Fep's for dinner; Mrs. S. and Mrs. J.G. sent by me for 2 Kamonias; came by way of Mother G's and got water; just as was fixing for bed 2 boys drove up and ask for drink, so just sat pail out side door and let them help themselves and "g" but they most emptied it, they thanked me ever so many times and said my but that water is fine.[90]

THE CENTRAL AND SOUTHERN GREAT PLAINS are home to some of the most violent summer weather in the world, hence the nickname "Tornado Alley." In this letter a Nebraska settler from Otsego, New York, describes to his brother the death and destruction caused by a massive tornado. Settlers unfamiliar with the terrifying tornadoes called them "cyclones" or "whirlwinds." They had good reason to be frightened, since many of their early homes were poorly constructed and no match for a tornado's power.

Grand Island Neb, July 10, 1871
Dear Brother,

This will inform you that we are all still alive. Hoping this will find you all well.

On the 6th instant, this country was visited by a whirlwind, rain and hail with considerable destruction of houses, grain, life and cattle. We could see and hear it, but it didn't come within 30 miles of our place and 12 miles from Bemans place. It was about six miles wide, the length is not heard from. Those that witness it describe it as a horable sene. The Express train was standing on the track at Lone Tree at the time. They say that they all went on their knees together with the old Catholic Priest. He says he saved the train. You will see by the papers, if you get them that accompany this sheet, but facts are not all put down.

In one instance of old Mr. Phelps, his house was takin up bodily and carried up nearly 100 feet high. They think he must of fell out. For when they found him, his head was in the ground up to his shoulders. He must have fell head first. The oldest girl is not expected to live. All the children was hurt. The girl was blown a mile. Mr. Phelps was a widdower, a Christian man.

It took some hogs up fifty feet and tore them to pecus. I think it must took the devil out of them. Our viliges are full of Eastern visitors. They say our crops excede all crops east. If we are [not] visited with enny moore of

Remains of a farmstead after a tornado in eastern Colorado

winds of devastations and grashopers, we can get out tolerable good crop, altho the air has been full of grashoppers for some days, but they don't light.

Write often. Love to all.

Affectionate Brother

S. Lamb[91]

MANY EARLY SETTLERS were unfamiliar with the long, often harsh winters of the Great Plains. Being caught unprepared compounded their suffering. This homesteader wrote to his cousin that the weather turned so bad, he had to burn timbers from his stable and house to keep his family from freezing.

Settlers who stayed on the plains quickly learned winter survival skills, such as having adequate supplies of food and fuel stockpiled before the first snowfall. Even today, many residents take winter precautions such as traveling with winter survival kits in their cars and keeping their fuel oil and propane tanks full.

Roanoke, Faulk Co. [Dakota Territory]
March 16, 1887
Dear Cousin,

I received your letter with five dollars this afternoon. I was exceedingly glad to receive it, I had about given up to ever hear from you. I could not imagine what could been the matter. I did not get a word from you. I am sorry to learn that Phebe is sick. Hope she will soon recover.

We have had a fearful hard winter from beginning til a week ago. I hope I will never see such a winter again as I was so unprepared and thousands the same. As good luck, I took a load of wheat early in the fall to Aberdeen to the mill, and that was our main support, but it is about used up now. We had one hog & that is all gone. We had no potatoes nor no kind of vegetables whatever. We have been weeks without tea nor coffee. We had only four pounds of butter this winter, had no means to get anything. We suffered fearful from cold. Had no coal to burn, had to burn straw and horse manure. They call it horse chips and that was scarce. As you may know David it was impossible to keep very warm when the mercury is down to 45 below zero.

There were days we couldn't go out the house with the blizzard to get straw. I was obliged to burn boards of the stable and overhead in the house so to keep us from freezing. Our house is very cold. I meant to fix it last fall but had no means. I suppose if I had done as many has, proving up on their homesteads, I might had money as well, but I did not want to mortgage my homestead. I would be required to prove up on it before I should get money on it. And not that I would be obliged to pay two hundred dollars to the government besides expenses.

This makes my second winter to live on my homestead. When I live 3 years on it, it will be mine and very little to pay on it. I shall be under obligation to go out and earn this summer so as to support my family and let the land idle. I have no money to buy seeds and only one horse. One of my horses broke her leg and another died a month ago. I have been very unfortunate. Hoping there is better day coming, I shall let Sarah write and finish it.

I remain,
Your cousin,
D. W. Williams
Give my respects to all enquiring friends. Write soon.[92]

Of all the winter storms that occurred on the northern Great Plains, the most notorious took place on January 12, 1888. The storm began on an unseasonably warm, humid winter day, picking up speed and muscle as it swept across the treeless prairie and turning into a blizzard with near-hurricane-force winds and subzero temperatures that rolled over farmsteads and settlements. The storm became known as "the schoolchildren's blizzard" for the number of children who were caught out in the storm and killed. This homesteader's family nearly perished in the blizzard, an experience that caused her to rethink living on the Great Plains.

Bloomington, Dak. Jan 23rd 1888.
My Dear Brother and Sister,

Your (Oh so welcome letter) of Jan 1st was received last week. We sympathize with you in the loss of your little innocent Darling. What is your loss is his Eternal gain. A sweet flower "Budded on Earth to Bloom in Heaven."

Dear Brother and Sister, I realize more and more every day the responsibility of raising a family and feel my unfitness for the sacred duties of Motherhood. We may awaken cords in those entrusted to our care. Cords that will vibrate through all Eternity either for good or evile. Oh let the example before our children be such as we would wish them to follow. I'm glad to here Ada is quite well again. Hope your healths may all continue good.

We are all real well this winter. Haven't had a good health of a winter since we came to Dak. Josie has a peculiar sore throat. Think it must be cronic enlargement of the tonsils. Have been very much enlarged for 6 weeks but not badly enflamed. He seems to feel well most of the time.

I suppose you have heard of the Blizzard that we had on the 12th of this month. Well I have seen the Dread of Dak. A genuine blizzard and am now ready to leave any time that we can sell. I will send you a paper soon. Oh if I could see you I could talk so much better (and faster) than I can write. I ought to have written sooner for I fear you have worried about us if you have heard of the storm. I fear it reached you also but hope you met with no loss from it. I want you to answer immediately for I can't rest until I hear from you. We were all spared but a great many perished during the storm. Oh, it was terable. I have often read about Blizzards but they have to be seen to be fully realized. We have been having a hard winter here.

On Thursday, Jan 12th Charlie started to go to the barn. He stopped and called "Sadie, Sadie." I stepped out on the porch. Said he, "The change has come we are going to have a thaw, it feels like a spring morning so soft and warm." I told him I hope it would warm up so people could get some fuel hauled. He went on to the barn to do up his chores. About 9 o'clock a young man, a neighbor of ours, came to take the children to school. We take them one morning, Mr. Switzer the next and so on. They send 6, we 3, to school. Charlie told him to leave the comforters at the school house as it might storm before night.

About 10 o'clock Charlie came in got his fur coat and scarf in a hurry, said he was going for the children as quick as he could get there, that the wind had changed to the northwest and had grown 10 degrees colder in less than an hour. I looked out and told him I was afraid he could never get there. Said he could get there now better than when it was colder. When he left the house I could only see him 4 or 5 rods away. Shortly after he left I went to the coal box which is east of the house about one rod. The storm was coming from the northwest. When I got into the wind I could not stand on my feet. When the wind first struck me it took me about 2 rods southeast against a snow bank. I tried again to reach the coal. Finaly reached the box and by hanging on to it I got to the other side where I could reach the coal. When I turned my head toward the storm I could not breathe. The wind was fearful. The snow so thick I could but dimly see the out lines of the house. I could not stand so crept over a bank of snow that had drifted around the boxes until I got out of the wind. Then got on my feet as best I could. I was getting so cold and numb while at the box I didn't know whether I could stand it to get back to the house or not. I then realized how easy it was for a person to freeze to death out in such a storm.

When I got in the house I could scarcely speak for a few minutes. I was so exhausted and out of breath. Then I realized what C. had undertaken to do. I knew that no living man could reach the school house and get the children home alive. Oh the agony of that hour no one can tell. The storm grew wilder colder and thicker every moment until it seemed to breathe nothing but Death and Death inevitable in its every gust. You could not see 3 feet from the window at times and not 6 feet ahead all day. And that was out of the wind on the east side of the house. In about an hour I heard a noise at the door. I almost flew to open it—there was Charlie. Chilled, and his face and eyes covered with ice. He could scarcely see. Had got lost coming back. He got out to unhitch and found he was in a patch of corn where he had stuck out cuttings last spring. Then he knew the well was not far off but didn't know in which direction to go, but started again and finally saw a board sticking up that he knew stuck out of the well. From the well he tried to go direct south about 4 rods to a hay stack and come to the east end of the barn 3 or 4 rods east of the stack. He thought he would have to leave the team two or three times but finally got them in the barn. Coming from the barn to the house, which is about 8 rods apart, he got lost and finally got to the outhouse so he reached the house from there. Aaron, I don't suppose there are 2 men in South Dak harder to lose than Charlie and his Brother Dave. At least they have that name and when Charlie couldn't travel, it was no use for any one else to try, as one of our neighbors has said, he saw he could not get back if he had got to the school house so he tried to get back home. The schoolhouse is northeast of us about one mile.

In the morning before daylight Charlie was up and started for the children and found them alright. Another, Mr. Shaw, had got there with breakfast for them all. During the storm the teacher (Charlie's brother David) and the scholars became so filled with electricity they couldn't touch one another. [Snow blasted by wind across ungrounded metal objects created high charges of static electricity.] Their coal gave out in the afternoon so they had to burn wheat that was in the house. The fire went out once and the last match started the fire for them again. A pretty close call.

There has been a great many deaths. There were two men found on the Reservation, one dead froze stiff sitting up, the other found walking around him singing and praying laughing and shouting by turns. Crazy. Had been out 26 hours but was not badly frozen. His companion had told him to go on if he could—the live man said no, if you stay I will stay with you and if you die I'll die too before I will leave you alone. He said they tried to follow a wire fence that led into town when they first found they were lost but could not breathe when near it, owing to the electricity. There were a number of others found dead trying to follow a wire fence. Near Scotland where C's uncle lives there was a school man and 18 children froze to death. They tried to get to a house a short distance from the school house. There was a wire fence led right to the house. In the morning the teacher and 9 scholars were found hanging onto the fence dead. The rest had got lost getting to the fence. North of us on Crow Creek one man was found standing up with his hand over his eyes froze stiff in the snow. Two men were found dead in a sod shanty northeast of here about 12 or 15 miles. Two men and three children froze near Armour, our nearest railroad town. A father went for his children to the school house and started back with them; all froze to death trying to reach their house. Another man went with him and also froze. I can't enumerate all the deaths we have heard of. Oh it was just terrible.

I guess I shall have to close for this time as we are expecting to go to Wheeler yet today visiting. It is the County seat 12 miles from here. Will be gone 2 days. This is a beautiful day with prospects of good weather now for awhile. A great many are out of fuel and are burning corn. It is 25 cents a bushel. I hope you will write soon.

Your loving sister,

Sadie Shaw

What are you doing this winter and how are you getting along financially and every other way? I would so love to know just how you are situated. It is hard times here. We have proved up and mortgaged our place to pay part of our debts. So we now have all of our personal property clear and if I have my way there will never be another mortgage put on a head of stock or anything else. We got 600 bushels of corn in the crib before winter set in so will not suffer for fuel, but will not burn corn unless we are obliged to keep from suffering. Have coal to heat 2 weeks yet. We will be so glad to get your pictures. We will certainly send you our pictures if we have them taken but can't get to the railroad this winter.

Love to all,
Sadie and Charlie[93]

HUMANS WEREN'T THE ONLY ONES VULNERABLE to devastation caused by a blizzard, as an unknown Colorado rancher describes to his parents. Unprotected cattle—unlike bison, which had evolved on the prairie and were able to withstand winter's temperatures—often died by the tens of thousands when storms struck. Even Theodore Roosevelt became disheartened with life on the Great Plains when he lost most of his cattle in northwestern Dakota Territory during the long winter of 1886–87. His stock starved and froze to death when deep snow covered the grass, making it impossible for them to forage.[94]

Wednesday P.M.
Dear Folks:

Must tell you about the biggest storm Colorado has had for twenty five years. Don't worry for its all over and the sun was shining today.

A family digs out after a three-day snowstorm in North Dakota.

Friday, Saturday and Monday we had hard winds. Monday night it all clouded up black, the wind died down and it began to lighten heavy in the northeast at first, then it became general.

About ten o'clock it was raining and it was still doing so when I went to sleep. In the morning the wind was howling and blowing as I have never heard it before. My windows were covered with snow, buried you might say. I opened the door and you could hardly see five feet in front of you. Burt's house was not to be seen and it isn't 60 feet between them. The air was full of heavy wet snow driven in solid masses, till you could not walk against the wind.

I got to Bert's house but it was a fight every step of the way. We could not make the barn, and the horses had to stand there all day, altho Bert did work his way down and get in some fodder thru the trap door. The barn was all but buried—drifts were here and there changing as the wind changed. There are drifts from five to twenty feet deep today, and the snow is half water so you can imagine what a lot of water will be running in a day or two. A man wouldn't live in that storm an hour. Bert said that "if a horse was tied to a post, it would be dead in less than an hour." Can you get any idea of the severity of the storm? I never expect to see one like it or want to.

This morning it stopped snowing about seven and the sun came out warm. We shoveled the buildings out and then went looking around. Over in Mule Creek they are hauling out the dead animals from the drifts. The creek is drifted full of snow and they don't know how many are buried there. Six big steers were hauled out of one place I saw. Three calves in another. The cows are calving now and that will mean a big loss for the Ranchers. Of Eppel's 450 head, they can only account for about fifty now. They broke fences and drifted here and there before the storm. More skeletons to lay on the prairies for the bone men [gathering bones for fertilizer]. Don't know how many thousands of dollars were lost by this big storm. Any stock out, if they didn't die, suffered terribly.

A man just came by looking for six horses who had broke out of his coral. Said his cow laid dead not fifty feet from the barn. The heavy wet snow alone was bad enuf, but it was that terrible wind that made the storm what it was.

We have got moisture enuf for crops now and this country ought to boom.

O'Leary is going to try to get to town tomorrow so will send this by him. Wonder if this storm hit Wis.

We are well and O.K.

Lovingly,

[name illegible—postmarked October 11, 1910, Reem's Ranch, Roggen Colorado, to Mrs. S. L. Reems, Lima Center, Wisconsin][95]

The Harvey Andrews family of Nebraska at the grave of their son Willie

Death's Shadow

Many of science's greatest achievements have been made in the fields of medicine and health care. Because progress has been so great and impacts so far-reaching, it is difficult to comprehend the health issues and medical care of Americans who lived a century or more ago. Vaccines were almost nonexistent. Drinking water and food were often unhealthy. Workplace accidents were more common.

Not surprisingly, in 1890 the average life expectancy in the United States was forty-seven years. It may have been even lower on the Great Plains because of the risks associated with everyday life. Settlers were subjected to the hazards of travel, farming, blizzards, prairie fires, and tornadoes. Childbirth was risky for both mothers and children.[96]

By far the biggest threat to survival was disease. Outbreaks of various ailments swept through settlements, killing children, the elderly, and the weak. Common diseases were "spotted fever" (typhus or epidemic meningitis), "lung fever" (pneumonia), measles, diphtheria, cholera, smallpox, whooping cough, and influenza. The trails to destinations on the Great Plains are littered with unmarked graves, especially those of young children who died from cholera or dysentery caused by unsanitary water and cooking conditions.

In the mid-nineteenth and early twentieth centuries, epidemics were common throughout the United States and the world. But living on or traveling across the open prairie—often without doctors and adequate supplies—made survival particularly challenging. Doctors frequently had to travel for hours to reach sick people, forcing neighbors to care for one another, sometimes with home remedies. Often, the remedies had little effect, and the human interaction furthered the spread of disease.

Winter on the northern Great Plains made it even more difficult to contend with outbreaks of disease. The weather interrupted travel for extended periods, preventing families from getting outside help and comfort. The result was that many people suffered alone in their household and watched family members die.

While far-reaching advances have been made in medicine, disease prevention, and medical care, many Great Plains residents today continue to struggle with access to quality medical care. As populations have declined in some regions, hospitals have closed and doctors have moved away. It is not uncommon to live an hour's drive or more away from a doctor or major medical center.

A YOUNG GIRL, Emma Kellogg, writes her grandmother to tell her of an outbreak of "spotted fever" that has made her mother seriously ill. What we know today as epidemic meningitis is easily and quickly spread by contact with nose and throat discharges from infected victims. It is often fatal.

Emma's mother, Sarah Ann Kellogg, a Quaker who had settled in Iowa in the early 1860s, struggled to add a note to her daughter's letter. She had contracted the disease while helping to care for friends who were ill. Sarah died the following month.

Correctionville [Iowa] Feb 18th 1863
Dear Grandma

I now sit down to write you a few lines to let you know that I have not forgotten you for I have not wrote in such a long time. I cant say we are all well as usual this time because ma is very sick with the spotted feaver. They all have the spotted feaver around here—they have it over to sioux city and every where else. One man over to sioux city was taken sick with the spotted feaver Monday and died Tuesday, so you may know that this is a very dangerous disease. But ma is getting better every day. When they are taken sick with this disease they are taken with the chills. I cannot think of any more to write at this time. write soon.

Emma to Grandma Strang

PS. Ellen has had the spotted feaver to but she hant been as sick as ma has been. I would like to know how Aunt Mary is getting along. I would like to see them all.

Dear parents, I have been sick 3 weeks with the spotted fever. I had been sick a week before Ellen [came] down with it. There is a child in the neighbor that has been sick 4 weeks & it lays just the same yet, neither dead not alive with the same fever & a young man that has been sick a month and cant turn himself in bed. Yet there is not well ones enough to take care of the sick. Morris has taken care of us all the time. Ellen can set up, but I am on my back yet. There has been a great many of the soldiers sick with the fever & a great many died at the city. We are coming back as soon as we get well. I thing Morris had better hold the office and not be drafted [into the army?] but he says he wants to go. John + Mary must not go back in the spring for I must see them. I am very tired so good bye, kiss [illegible] for me. love to all

Sarah

We don't want that money.[97]

In this letter from Minnesota, a homesteader writes his parents in Norway to inform them of the death from whooping cough of his young son Carl, clearly one of his favorite children.

Death and disease impacted nearly every early settler in one way or another, but children were particularly vulnerable. This letter writer suffered terribly: by 1900, he had lost seven of his children. In 1880, 246 out of 1,000 children died within the first year of life. Today the figure is 7 out of 1,000 in the United States.[98]

Luverne, Mn.
August 10, 1878
Dear Parents,

I have received your letter all right, Father, so I wish to answer it. As there has been much sickness in my house I have not written for some time—during the spring and summer I have feared losing some of my children, and it did so happen. The mild winter left much sickness among the settlers all around. There was scarlet fever, measles and whooping cough. Nearly all the homes were visited by one of these diseases, and it was the whooping cough that attacked my youngest ones—little Carl did not live through it. He died May 1st, about 14 months old and was buried May 5th. It was hard to lose that serious, loveable little boy, and yet I can say I was prepared for it as I had always thought he would not grow to maturity—his looks and actions were not of this world, yet I did not want to believe he would depart from us this early in life, then the horrid cough came upon him.

It is so strangely empty here since he left, as he was very dear to me and I could certainly say he was "flesh of my flesh and bone of my bones." God had other plans—and now I can look forward to seeing two small sons meeting me with open arms on that Great Day. I wish I could soon go there and join them as I am often tired of the confusion in this life. It is only the love and responsibility for my children that keeps me encouraged. But I am glad anyhow that I could keep little Astri, as she almost went the same way. Next to God's help, I can also thank the good doctor, that her life was spared.

The weather and crops look good and things seem to be maturing a month earlier than usual. Land has risen in value so I think I could get $2000 for the farm if I decide to sell. Around the country and in town there is much activity as we all are hoping the grasshoppers will not come—there is yet no sign of them.

Congratulations to you upon entering the golden age. May God grant that I will hear from you for many years yet.

Greet everyone.

Big Ola[99]

E. H. Cotton's husband had to leave their Dakota farm to find work to help support his family. In her letter she updates him on the health of family and neighbors. Winters were particularly hard on the settlers' health. In small and often crowded homes, airborne diseases such as measles and whooping cough spread quickly. These diseases, combined with common winter illnesses like pneumonia, flu, and colds, meant that hardly a household was untouched by sickness. During the settlement era, measles was a leading killer—especially among children and the elderly. Today, due to vaccinations, there are fewer than one hundred outbreaks annually in the United States.[100]

Parker, S. Dak
March 16th 1889
Dear Husband

How are you this morning? It seems a long time since we heard from you. We are well with the exception of bad colds. Norman, Nettie, Gracie and Winnie have bad colds settled on their lungs; they are all getting better now.... I am still able to do about the usual amount of grinning.

Normans Evans' heifer had a calf last Saturday but had not milk and as we had had nothing else to give it, we fed it hay tea but yesterday it died.

Last Sunday morning Mr. Benson died of Pneumonia fever. There was a large funeral, the largest I have attended in Dak. There were 21 teams in the procession and three or four more joined us at Parker. The Grand Army boys were out and so many of the relations.

Yesterday we buried two of Helmeg Johnsons children who died of measles, a little girl aged between 3 and 4 and one six weeks old. The other three children that are left and Mrs. Johnson are all down with measles. Now Helmeg has them all to attend to, only has the neighbors to come in and help. Mrs Amonson is down with lung fever and the children are down with measles, only Mrs. Amonson has to do everything at Oddlands Homes. Ericksons, Knudsons all have more sick ones, measles and lung troubles. They have the measles very hard this winter. Mrs. Almonds were afraid for a while that they would lose their baby but they are all better now, as is also Binedrick Miners. But May has come home with her children who are just coming down. It seems as though the neighbors are having hard times.

We have reason to be thankful that the aflicting hand is not laid so heavy upon us but then he does not afflict willingly nor grieve the children of men. Hope the lord is keeping you safe and well. Its time to start to town and I must close

Lovingly yours
E. H. Cotton[101]

Factors such as the lack of physicians and the long distances required to assist the sick compounded the number of deaths on the plains. When the doctor mentioned in this letter finally arrived at Sara Sim's homestead, her son had already succumbed to complications from pneumonia and the mumps. Sara herself had just recovered from severe depression over the death of another son, during which, her husband wrote in another letter, she tried to mutilate and hang herself. As Sara makes clear in her letter, the death of a second child increased her feelings of depression and loneliness.

Unfortunately, this would not be Sara's last experience with a child's death. By the time she died in 1880, she had lost six of her children to death and disease in Nebraska.

Ottoe, Nebraska, May 19th 1864
Dear Sister

It is some time since we have written you. I do not recollect whether we answered your last letter and now I must communicate to you the sad intelligence that we are again called to mourn the loss of one of our children. Our little Frankie died last Sunday morning very suddenly. Some 3 or so weeks before, he had an attack of the lung fever and we had the doctor for him and he got better. A little more than a week before he died he was taken with what I called the mumps. Philly had just had the same complaint and was got better, was not much sick but it seemed to make Frank sick. However I thought he would get better in a few days. I kept him close and doctored him some, but he did not get along well. We thought we would send for the doctor, he did not come that day, and the next morning he seemed much worse and his father started directly for the doctor and was not gone an hour when Frankie died. O what a trial to lose another of our dear children so soon. We have now but two left—poor blind Philly and a little boy a little over two years old. We are left very lonely indeed, nobody but ourselves and two little children.

We rented the most of our land this spring but the [hired] man did not seem to be of much account and is gone away and we have it all on our own hands and have to get along the best we can. I would like to go east this summer but I don't see how we can possibly leave but I intend to go as soon as we can arrange our affairs to leave. Father is very anxious for us to come home this summer. I wish we could go but then we can't have things all our own way. We have not heard from home for . . . I feel very anxious to hear from them. I suppose father is very feeble. I do not much expect to see him again in this life.

Mr. Sim wrote to Willis several weeks ago on some business and we have got no answer. What is the reason he does not write to us? We got a letter from Mr. Herrick a short time ago.

Our love to you all. Write soon.

From your affcte Sister

S. M. Sim

P.S. Enclosed I send you my photograph.[102]

In this tragic letter, Montana homesteader Lulu Benjamin informs an acquaintance about the death of the birth mother of Benjamin's foster daughter, Dorothy. The mother, her husband, and child had been sheepherders living an isolated life surrounded only by the prairie, their flock, and a few dogs. Sheepherders, who often grazed their animals on the vast tracts of public lands unclaimed by homesteaders and other settlers, lived in sheep wagons. Fitted with permanent rather than canvas covers, the wagons had sleeping, kitchen, and storage areas. The family quite possibly fell victim to the influenza epidemic of 1918–20, during which one in four Americans contracted the disease and more than 650,000 died.[103]

March 14, 1919

My Dear Mrs. Hanks—

My son is going to town in the morning & I will make haste & write you the awful news about Dorothy's mother. You remember I told you that her mother married a young sheep herder & lived way over on the plains be-

A funeral procession of wagons makes its way across the Montana prairie, 1913

yond the sheep hills—they lived in a sheep wagon in a most primitive way. I had not seen or heard of her but once since Dorothy was married until last Sunday. The man who owned these sheep was here last Sunday & told us that when he went the week before to take supplies, as was his custom every two weeks, he found Dorothy's mother, her husband and a little child, all 3 dead in the wagon undressed in bed—evidently they had been dead some days & the coyotes (young wolves) had eaten their hands, feet and faces beyond recognition. The man said he went for help—dug a deep wide grave, lined it with sage brush & folded the dead in their bedding & buried them. This place is about 70 miles from us. There's no knowing what happened to them; suppose they died of the flu or perhaps they were too sick to protect themselves, & the coyotes might have killed them as the dogs & sheep had drifted many miles from the wagon.

It was up to me to write this awful news to Dorothy—she never seemed to have a certain real love for her mother but she was her mother just the same. I finished the letter this eve & I am still all broken up over it—with all our hardships we always have good care. Weather has been cold & raw here with much snow, but today the sun has been bright & warm giving promise of the wondrous growing time that I love so well.

My little girl Nellie is doing fine only so awfully timid—I hope you can find some castoffs for her sometime. Your busy war activities are now I suppose things of the past for your dear husband & children to be proud of. With best wishes and much respect I am

Yours very truly

Mrs. E. E. Benjamin

Alzada, Montana[104]

Capturing grasshoppers in Minnesota, as depicted in Frank Leslie's Illustrated Newspaper,
September 1, 1888

10

The Menace from Above

Of all of the demoralizing acts of nature, none were as cruel to Great Plains settlers as the grasshopper plagues. In certain years, especially during the 1870s, the insect pests inundated nearly the entire region from Texas to the Canadian border. The phenomenon was known as "being grasshoppered," and settlers, especially those whose incomes depended solely on producing crops, lived in absolute fear of a plague.[105]

The Rocky Mountain locust, a bluish-olive insect more than an inch in length, was responsible for the majority of the plagues. Native to the foothills of the Rocky Mountains and river valleys of Montana and Wyoming, it foraged on wild natural plants and grasses. When the prairie was plowed under and replaced with crops such as corn and wheat, the insects readily made the switch to new food sources.[106]

During plague years, grasshoppers hatched out of the ground in the millions, ate until their wings were fully developed, and then lifted off and rode thermal air currents. Randomly dropping down on farm fields, they would resume their destructive eating and lay their eggs. Traveling in huge swarms, they resembled a large glittering cloud when the sun backlit their translucent wings. Sometimes the swarms were miles long and blocked out the sun. Settlers closely watched the grasshoppers' movements, hoping and praying they would not land on their fields. (Outbreaks of other insects, like crop-eating beetles, crickets, and worms, further complicated the settlers' lives.)[107]

When grasshoppers alighted on a field or homestead, they voraciously ate everything in sight, including the wood on the sides of houses and the clothes worn by the men and women trying to battle their invasion. To make matters worse, because moist soil conditions produce microorganisms and fungi that damage grasshopper eggs, the massive Great Plains outbreaks often coincided with periods of drought, compounding the hardship for settlers. Grasshoppers caused so much destruction in certain regions that some early settlers starved to death for lack of food. Others, faced with the prospect of starvation, ate grasshoppers to stay alive.[108]

Repeated grasshopper outbreaks led the governors of Minnesota, Nebraska, Missouri, Iowa, Illinois, Kansas, and Dakota Territory to meet for two days in Omaha, Nebraska, in 1876 to develop strategies to combat the plagues. While various ideas were floated for "counteracting the evil," including the far-thinking notion of protecting birds that fed on the insects, the governors acknowledged that little could be done to stop the attacks once they started. That recognition ultimately led them to put the future of their states in the hands of God. The governors' final act at the meeting was to pass a resolution urging people to "offer up special prayers in their respective churches for deliverance from this great enemy."[109]

Although grasshoppers continue to damage crops on the plains, apocalyptic attacks such as those that occurred during the settlement period have not been experienced in recent times. The Rocky Mountain locust became extinct in the early 1900s, perhaps because grazing and plowing disrupted its breeding sites.[110]

In this 1874 letter, the unwelcome sight of a grasshopper invasion greets a rural Minnesota minister returning from a trip. As the letter suggests, successive grasshopper attacks made it difficult for settlers to survive economically or even to ward off starvation. Although they might wish and pray that the swarms of grasshoppers they often saw daily in the skies would land elsewhere, they knew that if their hopes were realized, a neighbor would suffer.

July 4, 1874
Reverend J. H. Sieker
St. Paul Minn.
Dear Brother,

On the 12th of June I arrived, thanks to God, in good health and spirits and renewed vigor at my dear home and found wife and children well. But what a destruction! had the army of God completed meanwhile. Nothing remained on my forty acre wheat field. Oats, corn and potatoes covered with grasshoppers and what they did not devour, the caterpillars and other vermin eat up, that followed upon the heels of the former.

At the commencement it seemed as if God in his infinite grace would make an exception with some; but visiting my congregations a few days afterwards, to look after families of whom I expected that they were suffering, I found enough of them who had no bread and I divided what I had on hand amongst 12 families to whom it came like a Godsend. I found also a number in both congregations, which were as yet joyful and hopeful in looking over their splendid wheatfields, and their joy reached in the hearts of their bereaved neighbors. But the dear Lord did not want to make any exception, for when the "grand army" was almost ready to march forward towards the South into Iowa, then they came in such masses through the air that the Sun was darkened. Joyful and hopeful that they would pass us and pitying at the same time the country where they were going to, we at once saw our hopes destroyed, for the Lord ordered them to swallow up also the few fields in our neighborhood which had been spared up to this time.

In what masses and with what fury they fell over the wheat I cannot describe. Hard, very hard it is for a great many people, who are near to despair, having hoped that they would be spared this year, they now see all again lost. One of those that had again lost all told me with tears in his eyes that the bread I saw on his table was the last loaf he had in the house and that had been borrowed; but how joyful shone his eyes when I gave him $4.00, which he took as if they came out of the hand of his heavenly father—So has the Lord overlooked not one in his punishment.

All the 60 families in my two congregations, of whom the greater part are here 1, 2 & 3 years without means, yea many of them who came here poor with many little children have not had one harvest yet, but have made their living by working for others, but now they are stricken down entirely. To earn anything here is an impossibility. Before fall they will have to harvest hay for the winter, and some who could go and earn something as farm laborers have to plow their fields, which look like wild prairies, if anything is to be raised next year.
Respectfully,
Reverend A. Kenter
Lamberton Redwood County Minn.[111]

THIS FARMER'S LETTER reports on grasshopper outbreaks in his county to Iowa's adjutant general, the state official responsible for trying to help those who were impacted by the plagues. States undertook efforts to help farmers survive the hardships associated with grasshopper attacks, in some cases gathering and distributing food, clothing, and seed. Congress also appropriated money for food distribution to settlers in need.

The economic effects of grasshopper plagues started a relationship between agricultural producers and the government that continues to this day. The federal government has provided billions of dollars in disaster aid to help farmers and ranchers survive various environmental calamities on the Great Plains.[112]

Hosper, Sioux Co, Iowa
July 21st 1874
Dear Gen,

Yours of the 10th is recd.

The Hopper came upon us Sunday the 19th in countless millions. They ate our crops at a fearful rate Sunday Evening. Monday it rained all day & they done but little damage. Today, Tuesday, is damp & cloudy they are on the ground & much inclined to eat. Think they would leave if the wind was in their favor. They are going South; if they stay many days our crops are gone.

Yours Truly
William Pursel[113]

GRASSHOPPERS WERE UNPREDICTABLE — no one knew how long they would stay in an area, what fields they would attack, or where they would fly next. Sometimes they consumed the crops in one field and barely touched those in the next. On other occasions, they would eat everything within miles, leaving only when nothing remained. John William Gardiner, a school-teacher who lived near Winchester, Kansas, recorded the daily movements of the grasshoppers in his diary during the summer of 1875.

Sat. May 22. Very warm in the morning and kept it up all day. The Thermometer stood at 101, they said, though I think that is rather too high. Saw the Grasshoppers on the move out of the rye & they were going N. W. & W. in front of the house. These were very thick, going right down into the wheat, but they are leaving it as fast as they come in, so it remains the same. In the evening were on the fences & were thick. Got the Register today.

Sun. May 23. A fine day but stayed at home all day & straightened out the Register. And also killed some G's as they were hopping around thick & in every direction. We killed about a bushel and still they were thick in the yard. P Dick and Vanderpool came down in the evening but did not stay long. Went to bed early. Cap came home 11 o'clock. . . .

Sun. May 30. A fine day, but I felt very tired & stayed at home all day. Read Wordsworth's Poems when I was not asleep. Went down in the Timber in the evening and saw lots of G's & came back through the rye and [they had] damaged it considerably. Then I went back into the rye. They were thick in that, & were eating the heads some & taking the corn in places.

Mon. May 31. A fine day & the G's are on the move & eat, and the people are badly scared. In some parts they have taken things clean & the farmers are preparing to plant again. They are dying in some parts from a little worm. After they are dead you can take the worm out & it looks like a meat

Grasshoppers waiting for the temperature to rise, Marshall, Minnesota, 1930s

maggot. Though I haven't seen any myself with the worm in them but have seen the D. G & the worm.

Tues. June 1. Lots of Grasshoppers and they are on the move & eat considerably. The people are not ploughin' much on account of the hoppers, for they eat [more] on corn that is ploughed than they do on that which is [not] ploughed on account of it being cooler & they like to stay in the ground which is cool.

Wed. June 2. Cool weather for this time of year. Last year we had some warm weather before this time but no G's. But they are plentiful this season and they are doing lots of damage, and if I ever had the blues I have them now. Did not go to Lodge for we had visitors & could not go very well, and feel kind of tired anyway....

Sat. June 5. Went up into the field to take a look at the hoppers' damage and found they had not taken the corn much, but had hurt the oats on the edges badly. Yesterday evening was the first that we saw them shed [exoskeleton]. They were hulling out rapidly though Bud found one. I think in a week the larger portion will be shed off.

Sun. June 6. This [was] a fine day for Hoppers hatching and Tommy and I went out in the rye and they were shedding off in great numbers. In the afternoon went to see my Girl for the last time, at least for awhile, for she is going away tomorrow. I found her waiting for me and she look as nice as could be. We had quite a nice time all to ourselves, but of course I could not stay always.

Mon. June 7. Was a fine day with not anything of importance to write about. The G's are not on the wing to day but are winging out very rapidly, and I think they will begin to leave in two or three days and they may go sooner. They have taken quite a number of fields of corn without leaving much if any and the farmers look rather blue.

Tues. June 8. Warm and nice, and about 10 o'clock the Hoppers began to fly. Went over in goodly numbers and those who were out doors most of the day say that a good many let down, but I think not as many as left, though I was only out a few times during the day.

Wed. June 9. Wind from the South West and before noon the Hoppers began their North Westward march—which is their general course. They light down in places. But I have not seen many come down and I don't think many will, though it is only guesswork with me.

Thurs. June 10. Wind from the South West and blowing like smoke, and the G's whirling in North Easterly direction, and in great numbers. Rode down [to] Cay Hinchman's and he said [they] were cutting his corn very [badly] and he thought he would have to replant nearly all corn ground if they kept on as they had before....

Mon. June 14. Nothing of importance transpired to day to write about, only the Grasshoppers are still on the move and are cutting in places the corn very badly. Nevertheless, I think there will [be] some corn left [in] some vicinities. It seems they are more ravenous in some districts than others.[114]

SETTLERS IMPLEMENTED IMAGINATIVE TECHNIQUES in an attempt to defeat or, at the very least, control the grasshoppers, attacks. They tried to burn and smoke them out and, as mentioned in the letter below, drive them into ditches filled with water and oil by using bolts of cloth to direct their movement. A variety of machines were even invented and tested, including devices pulled by horses that rolled through fields and supposedly scooped up the insects.

In spite of the creativity associated with these efforts, they, like many technologies designed to control or alter nature on the Great Plains, proved ineffective. The Missouri entomologist to whom this letter is addressed, in addition to his work on insect control, had investigated using the Rocky Mountain locust as a food source. While he found locust legs and wings to be "somewhat irritating to the throat," he noted that if the heads, legs, and wings were carefully removed before boiling, they made an "excellent fricassee" when cooked with "a few vegetables, and a little butter, pepper, salt and vinegar."[115]

[May 1875]
[To the Missouri State Entomologist]

The locusts are taking every green thing as fast as it appears above the ground in this part of the country, say ten or twelve miles from the river. Beyond that I am told there is little small grain, vegetables and corn. Most of the country shows as little sign of vegetation as it did in March, except the trees. All small fruit is gone, they have even eaten the weeds. We are rebreaking our land to sow millet and Hungarian grass and plant corn for fodder after they leave. If we can't raise something in this way this section will be destitute of anything to eat for man or beast. The question is, what shall we do? But few men have money enough to buy corn to do them until they raise another crop.

I fully believe if we had commenced in time we could have saved our crops by killing them. I tried my best to convince the farmers in my neighborhood but could only get a few into it. I am sure I have killed more than was hatched on my farm. My plan is to dig deep ditches along the fence in their run with a deep hole at each end of the ditch, into which they pile up and kill each other or smother to death. Holes bored with a post augur is a very good plan. In order to collect them in the ditch, I took forty yards of domestic [cloth], cut in the middle, made two wings like a partridge net, tacking to stakes every ten feet. Start at one end and stake down at

Ephriam Swain Finch demonstrating how he fought grasshoppers in the 1870s (image retouched by photographer)

each corner of the ditch slanting inwards, fit down well to the ground so they can't crawl under; this conducts them to the ditch; get ahead of them when they start to travel. I have tried many plans but this is the best. Coal oil will kill them; a shallow ditch will do with water in it, and a pint of coal oil poured in when the ground will hold water.

    Mr. R. Bottom
    Rockport, Missouri[116]

SETTLERS DEPENDED ON GOOD CROPS for their economic future. Sometimes they desperately battled the grasshoppers to the point of personal exhaustion. While farmers occasionally limited the damage caused by the insects, most often they lost their crops. This Minnesota letter writer saved half of his crop but lost all of his potatoes and a field of corn. Grasshopper invasions, successive crop failures, declining health, and losing a house to fire eventually spurred him to move to Colorado and later to Montana.

Rapidan [Minnesota] May 25, [18]77
My Dear Brother Sandy

    I thought I would write you a small note to let you know how we are getting along. We are all in very good health except father; he is not very well this Spring. The Babys and Emma are well. My health never was better and it is a mighty good thing that I am well for we have got the grasshoppers to beat the deuce. They have hatched out on Derbys Breaking [newly plowed field]. He sowed it and they have eaten of his wheat almost all of it and have been moving over onto our wheat in millions.

    I never worked so in my life. We get up at four in the morning and work as long as we can see fighting them. I have worked now nine days burning them and ketching them. I have found that by building a wall of straw all along our north fence we have stopped them from coming in. But there is a great many in already, but I think we can ketch and burn them. We have burned and caught many bushells. There is nothing but a stench of burned hoppers in my nostrils all the time but I am going to beat them, yes sir and beat them bad to. I will hang on to them with Bull Dog Tenasity. If they go across the field I go with them with fire and nett. So you see how it is. Crops never looked so well here as they do now. Why man talk about the seat of the war it is right here. If you sit down on the ground they will eat the seat out of your pants. But I think we will beat them. Well I am tired and must go to bed, it is past 10 Oclock. Will send you Donald and Sandy pictures in this. Write soon. Good by from your afectionate Brother

    David B Christie[117]

Struggling farmers wait at a Nebraska railroad siding for relief supplies to arrive.

11

The West Is No Place for Faint Hearts

The struggle to survive economically was the common thread that linked every Great Plains settler. Those who endured did so through hard work, perseverance, and frugality. (The preference for weak coffee today among many residents may stem from their ancestors' habit of reusing coffee grounds multiple times.) Many of the survivors were also blessed with a certain amount of luck, undergoing fewer farm- or ranch-breaking events such as drought or grasshopper outbreaks than their neighbors or counterparts in other locations.

During times such as the 1870s, when economic hardships most severely afflicted people living on the Great Plains, states such as Iowa, Missouri, and Kansas organized relief efforts to help struggling settlers. Citizens in other parts of the country assisted by sending money and clothes through churches and other relief organizations. While this practice is common today, these earlier relief efforts were one of the first large-scale attempts to provide charitable assistance to people living in another part of the country. Family members also did what they could to help relatives living on the prairie, usually by sending small loans and articles of clothing.

Unfortunately, most of these efforts proved to be too little and too late. A large percentage of the people who moved onto the Great Plains under the Homestead Act deserted their farms before "making proof," that is, before completing the term of residency, house construction, and acreage planting that would make the farm theirs. Even many who bought established farms or land claims from the railroads ended up abandoning their property because they could not make the mortgage payments.[118]

For those who persisted, the day they made proof to the government or paid off the note to the mortgage company was a special occasion. It not only signified land ownership and financial independence but also demonstrated that they were survivors. They had the will, the fortitude, and the means to endure what the Great Plains were capable of handing out.

But those who stayed would be tested again and again, as would their children and grandchildren. Like the vast sunsets, hard times would always return to the Great Plains. The Dust Bowl of the 1930s—referred to as "the Dirty Thirties" for the amount of windblown dirt that darkened the skies almost daily—pushed thousands of farmers and ranchers off the land. So did protracted regional droughts, high interest rates, and low commodity prices in the 1970s and 1980s.[119]

Even today, unstable commodity prices and drought plague farmers and ranchers of the region, many of whom are descendants of the original non-Indian settlers. Huge tracts of land in some areas are slowly being depopulated, towns boarded up, and farm and ranch houses abandoned as the forces of nature, coupled with uncertain agricultural programs and low commodity prices, continue to take their toll. This issue perplexes government policy makers, social activists, and religious leaders who struggle to protect the livelihoods of those who live there while balancing the constant need for costly federal disaster aid, social support, and farm programs.

WITH CROPS REPEATEDLY DESTROYED by drought and grasshoppers and with nowhere else to turn, a homesteader and veteran of the Civil War in this 1873 letter asks the governor of Iowa for help to keep his family from starving or freezing to death. He was joined by thousands of others faced with similar hardships. Although states had limited resources, they often responded by gathering and sending food, clothing, seed for planting, and, occasionally, money.

Nov 21st 1873
Governor of the State of Iowa
Dear Sir

I write to you to let you know our poverty. I have lived on my Homestead most three years and have given up a number of times that we must starve or freese, but we have strugled through. But the time has come that I cannot see my way through and ask help from the state. The grasshoppers have ruined our crops so we have nothing to get clothing, provision or fuel. Myself and family consisting of wife and seven children are destitute or close, to [where] our house is cold and my children are sufering severely. We have a little flour and when that is gone I know not where the next is a coming from.

We have gout a quarter section on section 2 in Obrineer township 97, range 42, south west quarter, a beautiful home and I hate to leave it. I have 80 ackers broke ready for a crop next spring and not a curnel of seed wheat to sow. I have no friends nearer than york state. I was a Volentear from New York and if I cannot get help from this state I will have to call on the president for help. [It] must come from some where. Uncle Sam gave me my farm for searving in the army, now I want him to help me through. I will state some little instances. Two years ago this winter we layed in bed two days and three nights in sucsesion and had nothing but roasted corn to eat. It was in one of these fearful storms, Our house had two feet of snow on the floor and had drifted through the siding till the sides was white. We had nothing to burn but green cotton wood. We thought we must perish last winter. We see naerly as bad and what will come this God only know. Please write if we can have eny help from the state and what we must do to obtain it.

William Lyle[120]

BETWEEN GRASSHOPPERS AND DROUGHT, it was not un-common for settlers to have several bad crop years in a row. After five bad years, coupled with the loss of his sister and a number of his children to disease, this immigrant living in Minnesota writes his family in Norway telling them that he is tired of the struggle and often longs to leave this world to join his deceased family members. He adds that he is considering selling his farm to get out of debt and moving west to Dakota Territory.

Ironically, many settlers believed that the answer to their economic woes was to move farther west and start again, not realizing that the region had even less annual rainfall. Ulti-mately, this settler continued the struggle to stay on his farm and became moderately successful. He donated a portion of his land for the construction of a church.

Luverne [Minnesota]
Jan. 2, 1879
Dear Parents and Siblings

You have no doubt waited a long time to hear from me, and it shows how unthankful I am when I do not write, especially as I usually am well and could be writing. It may be that these lines will arrive to find that one of you has gone on to Eternal rest, or become so sick in body and mind that you do not remember me. I have had a fear that this would be my punish-ment for neglecting you. I would so gladly turn all of this responsibility over to God but as long as He continues to give my fingers the needed strength as well as free will, He must intend that I should carry on. . . .

Here is very little joy; but what is this earth's trial compared to the joy that awaits us? We need to walk cautiously, looking upward, waiting to be set free. I am often tired, and wait with longing to leave this world and go there where I have several loved ones, including my two little sons who wait for me. I hope we can all assemble there.

I suppose you are aware that my life is very heavy, it is only my children that keep me going. Maybe it is meant to be that way so I can be more free when the time comes. It was a great sorrow to lose little Carl and then my dear sister left this world so suddenly; the only consolation is knowing they are better off than we. May God be merciful to all of us who mourn her loss. Most likely brother Ole has written about her death so I will only tell about my own things.

We have had five bad years so the worry of feeding my family has weighed heavily on my mind. Yet we should not complain as long as we do not suffer real hunger and want. However, we have come into some debt and for that reason I have considered selling. I could get $1800 or $2000, which would pay off the debt with some remaining for a fresh start. So I have taken 320 acres of land fifty miles further west, in Dakota territory. But I do not know if the sale and the moving will take place because it is no easy thing to get a farm sold after these bad years. Some time this winter I expect brother Ole to come west so we can discuss this matter. It is about

A farm sale during hard times in Nebraska, about 1900

140 miles for him to come but by train it takes only 24 hours. The railroad now extends 30 miles past us—to Sioux Falls by Sioux River where I have my new claim, though my land is farther north on that river. There is some talk of another railroad coming through this country—it would run north-ward and if there were two railroads working it is possible the land prices would go up. We have had a beautiful fall which lasted until mid-December, but it has been very cold since and I now have two sick little boys.

There has been much Diptheria (the Trondheim throat sickness) over in our town and several children have died thereof. I am afraid it may have also come into my house as Tollef and Niels were in town on New Year's eve. But I hope God will let me keep the children I have left—yet, may his will be done. Should there be any change in matters here I will let you know.

Among those around here with whom you are acquainted, there has been no change—all are well and going on with there work. Ole T. Opsata and Margit Opsata have sold their land to Tosten and Niels Opsata so now they (the former) must be cared for by their children. Ole T. Bergh sends

his greeting—he is well and happy. Ole H. Helling greets you, but he is not satisfied here, yet. If he gets his land sold he wants to go back to Norway—it is uncertain that will ever happen. Greetings from Ambjorg—she is with us now but is going back to town again. She speaks English now so manages well wherever she goes, and seems more content now. She is a real help to us when she is here and this is needed because Anne is not always well.

I am wondering if you got the letter I wrote last June as I have not heard from you; but possibly your letter is on the way; and if not I hope to hear from you soon.

Live well, all of you and may God be with you, adding spiritual and physical blessing this new year.

Greet all who wish to hear from me and especially I greet you.

Big Ola and family

Kristi, won't you write to me some time? Today, Jan 4, the boys are better. Ole is nearly well. They think there is healing in the red cap you sent. Ole slept in it last night and Tollef has it now so I hope he also gets well.[121]

OLIVER T. JACKSON, the founder of Colorado's African American Dearfield Homesteading Colony, writes to the author of an article that helped to spur settlement, updating him on progress at the colony. So named because the agricultural fields were "dear" to the colony's early settlers, Dearfield was established in 1910 by Jackson, a disciple of Booker T. Washington. Even though its original inhabitants struggled to eke out an existence, their hard work eventually paid off, as he describes in this letter. By 1921, Dearfield had approximately seven hundred residents, with assets of nearly a million dollars. The success was temporary, though. The Great Depression and the accompanying drought and grasshopper plagues caused the colony, as well as many other dry-land farming operations, to collapse. In the end, only Jackson remained, living in Dearfield until he died in 1948 at the age of eighty-four. Today, the colony is on the National Register of Historic Places and efforts are under way to preserve its remaining structures.[122]

Denver, Colorado
December 5, 1918
Mr. W. J. Harsha
Kremling, Colorado.
My dear Mr. Harsha,

Since I last made you a statement of the progress of the Dearfield settlement in 1915, we have made a most wonderful progress for tenderfoot homesteaders, as only about seven out of sixty were farmers. Up to 1916 it was hard striving and it looked at times as though we would not make it as we had not yet made a marketable crop.

We would get together, talk the situation over and agree to hang on and stick together and give it another trial. Out of the sixty families all but seven have stuck it out. Now that our success is assured, how glad we are and the seven quitters are very sorry. Some have returned to see how we were getting along and said that they could scarcely believe that Dearfield is the same place where we had started.

We have fenced in our lands and have over 100 miles of fencing. We have improved our houses, barnes, tool houses and corrals. There was a time when I could count all of the stock and poultry in the settlement by naming what each one had. Now we have hundreds of horses, cows, pigs and poultry by the thousands.

In 1917 we had our first marketable crop of potato, beans, corn, watermelon, cantelope, pumpkins, squash, onions, turnips, cabbage, tomatoes, oats, rye, alfalfa, and native hay. This year added new life and inspiration to the farmers and in 1918 they have done themselves proud as their marketable crop and stock will exceed $50,000 and we will have plenty to carry us over.

The farmers have done their bit in war contributions having sent five husky lads from the settlement, subscribed for $950.00 in war stamps and bought $1000.00 of Government Bonds besides other contributions to the Red Cross and other war activities. And they have boasted that they had a man and woman with a hoe behind every Black mother's son of Colorado who was carrying a gun at the front fighting for Uncle Sam's democracy and praying at night that God give them strength, sunshine and rain that they might raise enough product to feed them and return our black boys alive, crowned with enough honors for their brawn and fighting grit, to warrent Uncle Sam being democratic enough to go around and reach the struggling Negro of Dearfield and other places.

The moral and religious standing of the settlers is above the average and their praise during the strenuous war times would make the Kaiser hang his head in shame and have quit long ago if he could only have hear them.

From the sale of their crops this year they are buying better horses and tools, improving their homes, buying new furniture, pianos, phonographs and automobiles. We now have six pianos, twelve victrolas and four automobiles and one truck in the district. Ten of the settlers have gone together and bought a thrasher and paid for it out of thrashing of their own beans at 25 cents per bushel and have one thousand dollars worth of thrashing awaiting them for their neighbors and white settlers near the settlement.

Since there is no more government land within 20 miles of the settlement for homesteading, I am giving all of my attention to the building up of the town. We had our plans all laid last spring to build fifty houses and bring in fifty farm families from the south, but the cruel war came and emigration from the south was stopped.

There is about $40,000 worth of farm work in our vicinity that is being done by Japs and Mexicans. We are putting on a new campaign this winter to get in a few families next spring and bring that support to the town, as the settlers are now in a position that they can no longer go out to work from their own farms. Last spring they were offered as high as $6.00 per day at times but they had to refuse on account of their own crops. Their total acreage under cultivation and hay was about 5000 as they are getting in to the dairy business and it takes more hay for their winter feeding.

The dairy product will average $100.00 per week and they are making an effort to increase that to $500.00 per week next year. We have some new men coming in who are real farmers and who are buying out the weaklings and white ones. They have money to stock their farms with good dairy cows since they see from our pastures what fine prospects there are for that business.

Ten new families were added to the settlement last year and there is now a demand for several farms in 1919. Dearfield has now taken her place in the class of one of Colorado's farming centers.

All of the homesteaders have proven up and are now tax payers and producing to the commercial markets buying and selling. We have reached this point in eight year from the grass roots on virgin soil without capital or any appreciable knowledge of dry farming.

We have what is known as The Dearfield Farmers Association which meets every month, and some of the agricultural experts of the State Agricultural College of the County Superintendent meets with them. They send delegates to the farmers' congress at Greeley and Fort Collins. This organization has been very helpful to the farmers.

The women of the settlement are of an extimable class and are very industrious. Many of them could not resist the temptation of 30 cents per hour to work in the fields this summer and could be seen early and going late to and from the nearby farms. Their help was very much appreciated by their husbands and white farmers since their men could not be had.

I never could have accomplished what has been done in the establishment of the settlement and town had it not been for my wife who sacrifices untiring labor and patience to stay in the settlement and assist in encouraging and holding the people together. Mrs. Jackson is always sought for in times of trouble, trials, tribulations and joys. She is a Notary Public, the Judge on the jury in all cases civil, criminal, social and religious. She was a school teacher in Missouri for fifteen years and is thoroughly competent to fill the position as a leader in the settlement.

I cannot give too much praise to all the women of Dearfield for they have been faithful and co-operative and today my wife and I are rejoicing to see them all so happy and well contented for their sacrifices, labor and patience. It is often said by visitors to the settlement that they have never seen such contentment and happiness in any country community. Miss Louise Vincent a school teacher from Wichita Kansas who spent her vacation in Dearfield last summer said on her departure, "I hate to leave this freedom and contentment of Dearfield, it is worth it all."

New features for the farmers in 1919 are the tractors, trucks and grain thrasher. We have in a quantity of winter rye and some wheat planted. Many of the farmers have learned by experience that they get better results by breaking their ground every other year and are putting in their crops by disking and listing on the old ground. Their plan this year is to put in a lot of spring grain and break new ground for late crops.

The new features for the town are a fifty room hotel for summer visitors, an elevator and a creamery and canning factory.

Miss Odessa McCollough our school teacher and her co-graduate of Colorado College are planning for an Industrial and Agricultural College possibly a branch of some southern college.

A flattering inducement has been offered by one of Colorado's white philanthropists to build for us a large sanitarium to be supported by colored charitable organizations, churches, lodges and insurance organizations of the United States. Thus we are planning to occupy 800 acres of State Land adjoining the settlement on the west.

This coming summer we will make a special effort to attract as many tourists as possible. Out of some of them we hope to interest some of our wealthy Negroes to invest and establish us a substantial bank.

I want to say a word for our white neighbors and other friends. The white citizens are without an exception a very conscientious and respectable class and good citizens. Since we have been in the community we have gotten along very peacefully and our friendly relations are maturing with our progress.

We have made friends and established our credit with the commercial centers and I hear nothing but praise of our people's credit. They pay their bills and their trade is now very much solicited in person and thru the mails.

The Community fair this year was a grand success and was attended by more than 500 of our white friends from the county and from Denver.

We are under many obligations to the State and County officials for their many encourageing helpfulnesses: the County for the schools and bridges and other helpful needs in our early efforts: and the State officials of the five administrations I have had the honor of being messenger have all been in sympathy with my work in getting my people to go back to the land in Colorado.

Many of the officials have given personal help to individuals with whom they were personally acquainted. All have contributed to their churches and by visiting the settlement and droping a word of encouragement either from their experience or by some good advice. I am particularly indebted to the emigration board of the State especially so because under the secretaryship of Ed. Foster, editor of the Weld County News, in the colums of his paper the settlement has received much favorable comment, and advertisement. The emigration board has assisted by reference of colored applicants for land in Colorado, and with literature.

I am in position to know that any man colored or white coming to Colorado to make it his home, if honest and industrous will receive the full support of the officials and citizens of the state. Colorado lands and opportunities offer the best inducements of any state in the union for the poor farmer.

I want to thank you Mr. Harsha for your valuable help. Your article in the Southern Workman of March 1916 was of untold value to my work. That article was the means of attracting thousands of leading colored people to Dearfield and the plan of the settlement. Since your article appered in the Workman, several communities have been started in the United States either in rural districts or bordering large cities. Every Negro of prominence now who visits desires to see Dearfield, and we hope to make Dearfield the center of attraction for all people of the U.S. by our production and industries.

Thanking you for your interest I am.

O. T. Jackson[123]

WHEN A FARM STOPPED PRODUCING INCOME during hard times, the head of the household often left to find work. Families usually stayed behind. Railroad construction was a common part-time occupation for some, as was agricultural work in areas not hit by drought or grasshoppers. Others went east in the hope of finding jobs in the long-settled regions of the country.

Hard times also meant that many settlers, like this Dakota Territory farmer and his family, had to mortgage their farms and homes. This was a particularly bitter pill because they had come to the Great Plains in search of economic freedom.

[Roanoke, Dakota Territory]
December the 1st, 1887
Dear Cousins David & Margaret Williams,

As Dave is not at home—gone to Milwaukee since last Monday morning,

I answer yours in his stead. I sent it to him this evening so he will receive it the first of the week. He felt it necessary to avoid suffering this winter, as we did last, to go east to work until spring opens as there is no work or wages here to be had in wintertime. He too felt very discouraged for losing crops, horses and other things. Mortgaging in order to live at all has almost made him crazy.

My sisters has been very good to us in sending us warm clothes for this winter and we are warmly clad, have enough vegetables & flour for this winter, but our coal depends on Daves earnings unless he uses this [money?] you sent to buy it. I do hate to have him go away from home. I shall miss him so much.

I am very sorry of Phebes illness. Our little ones are well with an exception of a bad cold. Albert does the chores & goes to school this winter. I have no other paper so cannot write no longer letter this time. With respects to all the family, Fred and Sarah accepted, I remain,

Yours truly,

Sarah E. Williams

Dave spoke about writing to you just before he left home. I presume that you will hear from him soon. I have sent your letter to him. It is real hard work for him to write. Of late, weather has been 39 degrees below zero here last week.[124]

LIKE MANY SETTLERS, this Kansas farmer asked his friends and family members for financial assistance to help him stay on his farm until he could produce a crop. Despite the challenges facing him, he clung to the hope that his farm would eventually pay off. He even encouraged his brother to come and find a farm of his own, reasoning that his own difficulties were nothing unusual for a newly settled area.

Quinter (Gove County) Kansas

January 17, 1888

Brother Rob and family,

This is an answer to the Boys' letter. We are all well except very bad colds. We have had some of the coldest weather that was ever known in Western Kansas. We get along by the hardes [work?]. There is some talk among the people south of us applying to the governor of this state for assistence. God only knows how People is going to get through if the cold weather holds much longer, for coal is $8 dollars per ton. So you see if a man has no money he is compelled to go hungry and scant.

I suppose you think I am not telling the facts about this country. You can judge for your self. If in a country, no difference where it is, and have a failure, it will be to starve it through. I rote to Kate's folks at Champaign and ask them if they would help us a little. A little from each one would help us a great deal and they would not be damaged very much. And as soon as I could make a rase, I would pay them back. I also told them just how we was fixed and asked them as they were ample able to do a little. So in a month or 6 weeks they rote and [said] they was very poor and could not do anything at present, so we will starve it through. . . .

Rob, will you rite to Ed and Charley and see if you cannot get the Champaign folks to do something? I do not want to get up and leave my claim as some one will jump it and I will lose my labor and what I have put here. So by your riting to them and see what they will do, and a little help will hold my claim and we can live.

I am not the first man that has settled in a new country that has asked for a little help for I, myself, gave 1 bushel of corn and one dollar in cash for Western sufferers. If a man could find work at 50 or 75 cents per day, he could live. But no hiring is done and no work to get. I do not think I am mistaken when I say there was not corn enough raised in Gove to fatten the hogs.

Well, Rob, you said you thought this would be your last year on Joiner's farm. Now I only hope you will raise a good crop. Please come and see us and spend one month in the West and if you like it I will turn out the last teem I have to help pay you what I owe you and help Rob get a good home for his little flock. I am not going to blow the country up, just let you come and see for yourself and you, I know, will say it is as fine a country as God ever made.

Of corse, when Rene's father and mother and her grandparents settled in the new country where they did, they was scarce of money and had to live cheap. But now the old settlers of Ohio and Indiana, also Illinois, look on them when they got their land for $1.25 per acre. Now it is clear out of the reach of a common man's means from 40 to 50 dollars per acre.

Rob, you plese drop S. Smallwood a card and ask him what kind of a farm I have out here in Kansas. Plese do so and ask him about the country for you know S. Smallwood is no slouch of a man and what he says can be relyed on. A soldier has a big share here and the advantage over any other citizen. Your rights as soon as you are in Kansas are worth 800 dollars to you. You have 4 rights, or 160 each. That makes one whole section and that will growe your family well off in the corse of 10 to 15 years. And I am telling you the honest trouth. You and family look on the map of the U. States and you will find Gove County is near the center of the U. States. Now Rob, make your arrangements to come. Jacob Wick is coming after harvest. You rite him and see when he will come and then you and him come together.

Well, I must close for you see I have rattled off a long and not very interesting letter, especially if you are hungry. So for fear of any calamity in your appetite, I will bid you all good day. Kate and the little ones send the Best Regards and says for you to come shure.

Answer soon. Don't wait so long—

Asa[125]

DURING TIMES OF DROUGHT, selling the farm and moving away presented challenges. The large number of farms available for sale drove down land prices, making it a losing proposition to sell. As a result, many families simply abandoned their farms. Others stayed on the land and scratched out an existence—a predicament that caused some to comment that they were too poor to leave. In this desperate-sounding letter, a Nebraska farmer reports the large number of settlers fleeing the Great Plains because of drought. He himself had arrived in Nebraska from Michigan in 1880 and helped to supplement his farming income with carpentry work, building barns and schoolhouses. He stayed on his homestead until 1899, when he traded it for a different Nebraska farm, on which he lived until his death in 1907.

Supplementing farm income is common in rural America today. One in two spouses of farm operators holds a job off the farm.[126]

Butler, Neb. Aug 6, 1894

Dear Friends,

Today I will try to write you a few lines. This leaves us in usual good health, but in bad shape. Every thing is destroyed in the west part of the state by prolonged drought and hot winds. Thousands of people are leaving the state. 50 went through Kearney in one day, going to Mo. and Iowa and Ill. We have raised only about 5 bu. of wheat, not any oats, not any corn, not any potatoes, not any hay on this place. All we have to winter the stock on is the corn fodder, which is very small. We will finish cutting ours today, cut it with hoes and rake it up with horse rake. All we have to live upon is our cows and hens. The hens have stopped laying for want of feed. We have no grain to feed the cows and if they dry up, we have no hope unless the state helps the people. We will have no seeds to plant in the spring, no feed for the teams to work on. What we will do I do not know, but will try to face the future four-square and will not cross the bridge until we come to it. The fuel supply is cut off, which is corn cobs for the farmers. They have no money to buy coal with. We have a few trees about the place which we will cut. We are burning everything that will burn. All the fine brush, old corn stalks etc. I cannot picture to you just how things are.

Hope this will find you all well, with the blessings of the comforts of life. Love to all,

Goodbye,

B. S. Gitchel[127]

A Norwegian immigrant, luckier and more successful than the previous writer, reports to his brother that after twelve years in America, he has come to prefer his new life to the old one. He encourages his brother to make the crossing and not worry because "everything would work out alright for you just as for the million others who come to America every year." The fact that many Russian and European immigrant settlers came from the lowest economic classes, coupled with Old World laws that prevented a farm from being inherited by anyone but the oldest son, convinced many that they were better off on the Great Plains—however difficult the times.

Nutley [Dakota Territory]

August 5, 1888

Dear Brother Knudt Stavig,

I have received two letters from you for which I must thank you. I have not written a letter since I wrote to you so you must excuse me. There are many who lose my ink, pen and paper so I don't get to keep it for myself.

First, I will inform you that we are fairly well. Maren and I don't feel just right in health or humor, but we must be content with that since we are beginning to be old. I thank the dear Lord Almighty for the young sprouts that are flowering together with us. The children are growing like the field in the springtime. This spring we received another boy child who is named Edvin Odin. He is a big, good looking boy. Now there are seven in the family, all at home.

This summer I spent $200 on building. I have also bought a machine for seeding and a disc for $62, a cutting machine for $185. So I feel that things are coming together for me.

In your letter you asked advice about the farm—if you should buy it or not. I have answered that before and my answer has not changed. I cannot advise you but I would not go home and live around your stepfather even if I received the whole Knut farm for my own. I would hope that you would think more of your family than to bring them into such a situation. Dear Brother, evidently you don't feel too secure when you ask me for advice

The Wabel family's new frame, shuttered home in West Union, Nebraska, replaces a sod dwelling, a demonstrable sign of prosperity.

in such an important decision. It concerns your whole life and everything you own.

I want you to pay attention to what I am saying. I lived in Norway for 32 years and I have now lived in America for 12 years and I can see the difference. I think you would be doing the right thing by coming to America while you still have the money in hand. It will be too late when you have spent it.

I am not living in the most convenient place in America, but you must decide where you want to go. Don't decide not to come because you don't like where I live and feel that you have to come here. America also has problems just as Norway does, but there is a difference in their problems. You can be poor in America as well as Norway. In the beginning it is the worst, before you are situated and have made some money. You will always have food but you won't have a house and ownership.

You knew Anders Lodsberg's condition. You knew how little he had when he left home. You can't expect a man like that to be into money in such a short time. Anders and his family like it here. They have land and a house on the land so they are saved. And they have found food and drink as they need it. I'm glad that they are satisfied and happy. Dear brother, if you come everything would work out alright for you just as for the million others who come to America every year. You don't have such a big family that you will have any problem taking care of them in any way that you wish.

I have stated how I feel. You must decide the rest for yourself.

The grain looks beautiful so we should have a rich fall if nothing happens to it before the harvest. We have thunder and rain every other day so it is bad weather for drying hay.

The harvest is ready to start. We will start to cut the wheat next week and this week we are cutting the rye.

Here in this place where I live there is a lot of visiting among neighbors, especially on Sundays. You can not find many people home on Sunday. There have been many Sundays during the year when we have had 20 people around the dinner table. Today my mother and father-in-law are visiting. They are very glad that they came here. They are well and get around as they did in Norway. There are a lot of impossible things that can be possible such as when the old couple came to this land.

Dear brother, I understand that mother does not like what I write to you. You must tell her from me that everything that I have written is true. There is no right of inheritance here and no one takes over his parent's farm like a god. I understand that at home they have a lot to say about that and that's funny. Greet mother and say that if there would not be too much discord she could come with you to America if you come. She has been a big help to you. I still do not have a picture for her.

I don't have any more news to tell you other than that we have built a new church, and a school and at my house there will be no money at the bottom of the chest. That's what will happen to you, too, if you come.

I see from your letter that there has been a lot of weddings in Stavig, so it is no greener or dryer in Stavig.

Wishing you, brother and wife, luck through your traveling. Write back. Greet relatives and friends from me.

Lars A. Stavig[128]

ALICE NEWBERRY, *a Colorado schoolteacher and home-steader, writes her mother that she is going to make proof on her homestead. Living alone in a dugout, she has overcome*

Homesteaders pose on "proof day," in Murdo, South Dakota, 1907.

rodents, fleas, and difficult weather—and in the process become very savvy at the business of farming on the Great Plains. A single woman who never married, Alice moved to Denver and taught school after proving up. She retained ownership of her homestead, using the rental income to build the house in Denver where she spent the rest of her life.

"The Burrow" Stratton, Colorado
April 27, [19]09
Dear Mama:

I am enclosing a letter from Florence. I received it yesterday, and was, of course, very glad to hear from her directly. I sent her the pennyroyal [aromatic plant] because it is said to keep away fleas. Some people say that you can become so used to fleas that you won't mind them much. But I never could. We scarcely ever see them here now but I used to suffer so from them that I pity any one who has them to deal with, for I can't sleep nights nor do anything but scratch days.

School is over. I have sent in my annual report, and am through. In some ways I am very glad. But I shall miss that little monthly warrant.

My notice to make proof appeared yesterday (Saturday). I make proof May 29, instead of May 26, as the Receiver at the Land Office at Hugo has set that day for me.

I am very glad now that the cool weather and extra work that Mr. Tate had prevented my getting my wheat in before this last week. The few warm days we have had have caused every little Russian thistle seed to sprout and people who had their wheat put in in March when I wanted mine in say that the thistles are coming faster than the wheat, and will choke the grain out. But my thistles were all up an inch or so before Mr. Tate could begin on my land. Now all their little heads—millions of them, for their tiny stems stand thick together in clumps looking like the thick pile of a heavy plush or velvet—are turned under, and their roots yanked out in a way that delights me.

I was over to look at my "broad acres" last night after he went home from work. It looks very fine to see the low, level land, no weeds, and all so nicely disked and seeded. Its not anywhere near all in yet, and he hasn't begun on my barley. They can't come up again surely, those little thistles, and even if they do the warmer weather will give the wheat a better chance. Surely I will have a crop if there is no hail. Perhaps I'm dealing in "futures" but I hope my 33 acres of wheat will go 20 bus. to the acre. If nothing happens it will be 35 or 40 bus., for it does do that here when we have rain. But I'm counting on 20 only 660 bus. and one half mine means 330 bus. It will surely go 50 cents a bushel though I hope .80 or .90 will be the price.

20 bus. of barley means 20 acres sown. And I count on 30 bus. per acre

for that. 300 bus. for mine. It sold last year at 80 cents. Though of course if crops are good it can't be so high this year: say 50 cents anyway, and I hope to have enough to pay Uncle Glenn all I owe him on that note of last August, and then some over, a little sum anyhow. The ground is wet down to a depth of fifteen or twenty feet, and this low land does not dry so fast as the upland does. And a little rain this year will insure a crop. If again—there is no hail!

I hope to be home—to start June, if I can possibly manage it. I want to wait a week to see if my proof goes through. If it doesn't, but how can it help it?

My lettuce is up fine. I put in more radishes yesterday, and will put in a few onion sets today. I was going to wash but the wind is blowing so hard that it will whip everything to pieces. I want my clothes to stay on the line as long as possible when I wash. I've washed under so many adverse conditions and just when I could—so many times on cloudy days that I fear I'll never get the clothes to look white again. They need sunlight and all the bleaching agencies possible. I hope to-morrow will be a still, bright day. I will paper today instead—I must get my little house ready to receive those witnesses, and ready to refuse to receive snake. Last summer mice made holes in the walls. Remus, my cat, forbids such work this year, and there are no mice. So I hope any paper I put on this year stays whole. And there will be no expense save the work and the flour—$1.57 a sack. I won't use much however. When I said I would be home June 7, I mean if I don't take the Denver examinations. I can't come then until June 28. I can keep busy the weeks I must stay mending and repairing my clothes and studying, and so I hope the time will not seem long. My clothes are in pretty bad shape. I've had very little new and this winter has been pretty hard on them. I hope I can make what clothes I have fit to come home on so that no one will be shocked, or stand aghast at the appearance I present. I must close and go to work.

With much love to all,

Alice N.

I do hope winter is over. Surely it is, as it is nearly May.[129]

A Dakota Territory homesteader responds to a friend with frank advice on how to survive on the Great Plains.

Williamsport, Emmons County, Dakota Territory
April 10th 1885
Dear Ev

Yes I got the photo all right. Think that I would like Lizzie very much when we get acquainted.

About going West—if you can put up with any amount of inconveniences, hard grub, hard fare generally, work hard morning noon and night, stick too it—never let up, get out into some new country—start on the ground floor and hold your grip—be ready to do anything that turns up, you can make a success of it in the west. The west is no place for soft snaps—nor for faint hearts—All she asks from those who come is to stick by her, and those who stick win—I plowed, dug up stone—worked on the roads, hauled wood—worked in the hay fields—cooked and washed for my self, patched my own clothes, sew on my buttons, and expect to have to rustle for a couple of years longer—Money is scarce but grub such as it is, is plenty. My health is excellent—I have a good claim, think I could sell out for a thousand but expect it will be worth five in a couple of years and perhaps ten—but it will raise my grub and as soon as I can get enough ahead will put on some stock and then in a short time I can sit down and see my money grow—My honest opinion is that a young couple are foolish to stay east while land can be had for the taking and the taking is not going to last forever—Think of it—160 acres—you can't imagine what a nice little patch it is until you commence to plow half mile furrows—Much obliged for the papers. Did not think I had been so negligent about acknowledging the photo—Write again and give me an idea of what you think of doing in the West

Love to Lizzie—Aff

Ed[130]

"27 feet from mouth of tunnel to door"—the aftermath of a blizzard along the Little Missouri River, Wyoming, 1912

Dakota Land

We've reached the land of drouth and heat
Where nothing grows for man to eat.
The wind it blows with fervent heat
Until the folks are really beat.

CHORUS:

Oh Dakota land, Sweet Dakota land—
As on thy burning soil I stand
I look away across the plains
And wonder why it never rains
Till Gabriel blows a trumpet sound
And says the rain has passed around.

We have no wheat, we have no oats,
We have no corn to feed our shoats.
Our chickens are too poor to eat,
Our pigs go squealing down the street.

Our fuel is lignite, the cheapest kind,
Our women are all of one mind.
With bag in hand and up-turned nose
They are hunting chips that buffalo grows.

Our horses are of broncho race,
Starvation stares them in the face.
We do not live, we only stay,
We are too poor to get away.

These secularized lyrics of the hymn "Beulah Land" were handwritten on merchant's stationery from Mount Vernon, South Dakota, in 1895. Similar songs reflecting settlers' struggles with drought were named "Kansas Land" or "Montana Land."

Epilogue

As I drove across the northern Great Plains on one of my final research trips in South Dakota and Nebraska, I thought about how much had changed in 130 years. Traveling down U.S. Highway 14 at sixty miles per hour—two lanes of blacktop that had once been a trail that brought countless settlers into the region—I could traverse in ten hours what travelers journeying by wagons took a month or longer to cover. Along my route was a steady succession of towns, none of which existed when the early settlers had to find their way across the vast ocean of grass. While most of the towns were small, and some were even fading away, they were places to stop for food and conversation and to spend the night. Early voyagers longed for such opportunities during their journeys.

Most of the native prairie is gone, having been plowed under and farmed or grazed almost continuously since the settlers first arrived. The occasional exceptions are tracts of land that farmers and ranchers have placed in the Conservation Reserve Program, a federal program designed to reduce erosion and take marginal cropland out of production. These lands have been replanted with grass—including some native varieties—and with a little imagination I could occasionally get a sense of what it looked like when only grass was visible as far as you could see.

Early in the day, my route took me through the eastern edge of the Great Plains in Minnesota. There, rainfall levels are adequate to provide trees with an even chance of surviving, which means there are lots of them. They were planted in neat clumps or rows around houses and farm buildings. But as I traveled farther west that day, trees became scarcer. By the time I reached the Missouri River in central South Dakota, I had to scan the landscape to find them.

Small plows and other farm equipment pulled by animals were still visible along my route, but most had been relegated to lawn and garden ornaments, mailbox posts, and advertising for secondhand stores and coffee shops. Huge diesel tractors and plows as wide as houses have replaced the horse- or mule-drawn single plow. Too big to fit into most traditional barns, this modern farm equipment was parked under steel and aluminum sheds while the wooden barns of a century ago sat crumbling.

I also thought about what hadn't changed. Even with the trees, plowed fields, farmsteads, and radio and television towers on the horizon, I could still see the vast sweep of land that sometimes appeared to be without end. The sight was turned even more spectacular that day by an impressive sunset—a red ball of fire setting in a cold February sky—that made farm silos, fence posts, and an occasional windmill cast long shadows across fields.

Fickle weather has also remained a constant on the Great Plains. A good portion of the land was suffering the effects of a multiyear drought. Farmers and ranchers had sold off herds of cattle because they could not raise the hay to nourish them or afford to buy expensive feed. Small streams and prairie potholes were dry. Mudflats were even appearing within the reservoirs of the mighty Missouri River because of lack of rain and snowmelt.

The day I left St. Paul, the sky had been bright blue and the temperature unseasonably warm. By the time I had driven onto the Great Plains in western Minnesota, I was in the midst of a prominent winter experience— a raging ground blizzard with snow that had fallen days before being driven horizontally by a fierce forty-mile-an-hour wind. The eight-foot-high blur of snow had laid down a thick sheet of glazed ice on the highway. While I did my best to keep my ancient Land Cruiser on the road, a hard gust of wind coupled with the air current from a fully loaded trucking rig driving in the opposite direction caused me to lose control. I slid sideways into the ditch, hit a deep snowdrift, and then felt my sense of balance and equilibrium slip away as my truck rolled on its side.

I shut off the ignition and sat there for a few seconds, suspended horizontally by my seatbelt. Listening to the wind howl outside and seeing the snow quickly reclaim the scar my truck had created in the drift, my first thought was not for my safety or even to examine myself for cuts or bruises. What I thought about was the blizzard experiences of settlers and homesteaders—due, in part, to the fact that the rubber band holding together my three hundred–page manuscript had broken and the interior of my truck was filled with loose paper. My reflections were quickly interrupted when I smelled gas. I released the seatbelt and collapsed onto the passenger side window.

The character of the people living on the plains hasn't changed, I soon realized. As I struggled to push open my door against the wind, a farm wife and her daughter, who had taken the risk of pulling their car onto the shoulder of the icy highway, ran across the road to see if I had been hurt. When they saw that I was all right, they trudged through snowdrifts to the nearest farmhouse and called a tow truck. Meanwhile, a housing contractor pulled over and insisted that I sit in his truck, out of the wind and cold, until the tow truck and highway patrol arrived from towns that were, respectively, ten and fifteen miles away.

When the tow truck finally arrived, the farmer who lived across the road walked out of his barn and through the blowing snow to help hook a chain to my truck, tip it back over on its wheels, and then rehook it so it could be pulled out of the snowdrift and back onto the road. No one asked him to lend a hand, and it was obvious that he did not even know the tow truck operator. He just did it.

As my truck was being dragged out of the ditch, I walked over to the farmer and thanked him. I apologized for having interrupted his chores and for the embarrassment of having landed sideways in his ditch. He studied me for a few seconds, his blue Scandinavian eyes made watery by the wind and cold. Then he shrugged his shoulders. "Don't worry about it; it happens. It's just your turn, that's all," he said.

It *was* my turn. The same sense of fate and providence that existed among settlers in 1870, 1890, or 1910 exists today. The people living here know that you can do everything in your power to alter the landscape, to control your interaction with the environment, to dress up the prairie with farms, towns, and trees, but there is a recognition, especially among the more seasoned of them, that this is a place where you are constantly tested and never really in control. You live there with the understanding and the knowledge that some aspects of the Great Plains will never change.

Sources of Letters and Diaries

Notes

1. Loretta Fowler, *The Columbia Guide to American Indians of the Great Plains* (New York: Columbia University Press, 2003), 4. Most people consider the Rocky Mountains to be the western border of the Great Plains. I relied on historic documents, my own experiences, and a Nature Conservancy map of the Great Plains to establish my eastern boundary (see map on p xii), which runs from western Minnesota through central Iowa and Missouri to eastern Oklahoma and Texas.

2. Ian Frazier, *The Great Plains* (New York: Picador, 1989), 157.

3. Donald E. Trimble, *The Geologic Story of the Great Plains*, Geological Survey Bulletin 1493 (U.S. Government Printing Office), http://www.lib.ndsu.nodak.edu/govdocs/text/greatplains/text.html, accessed Jan. 5, 2003.

4. Donald Jackson, ed., *The Journals of Zebulon Montgomery Pike*, vol. 2 (Oklahoma City: University of Oklahoma Press, 1966), 27–28; Nebraskastudies.org, *1850–1874 The Challenges of Living on the Plains*, http://www.nebraskastudies.org/0500/stories/0501_0101.html, acc. Mar. 3, 2003.

5. Greatplains.org, *Atlas of the Great Plains–U.S. Mean Annual Precipitation*, http://www.greatplains.org/resource/atlas/atlas/prec.htm, acc. Apr. 19, 2000; Pennsylvania State Climatologist, *Decadal Precipitation Trends in Pennsylvania*, http://pasc.met.psu.edu/PA_Climatologist/decadal/decade.html, acc. July 23, 2002.

6. Frank W. Blackmar, ed., *Kansas: A Cyclopedia of State History, Embracing Events, Institutions, Industries, Counties, Cities, Towns, Prominent Persons, Etc.*, vol. 1 (Chicago: Standard Pub. Co., 1912), http://skyways.lib.ks.us/genweb/archives/1912/g/great_american_desert.html, acc. Nov. 11, 2004; Walter P. Webb, *The Great Plains* (Lincoln: University of Nebraska Press, 1981), 409.

7. Paula M. Nelson, *After the West Was Won* (Iowa City: University of Iowa Press, 1986), 7; James C. Olson and Ronald C. Naugle, *History of Nebraska* (Lincoln: University of Nebraska Press, 1997), 87–88.

8. Herbert S. Schell, *History of South Dakota* (Lincoln: University of Nebraska Press, 1975), 172.

9. General Land Office, *Homestead Law Circular*, Oct. 30, 1862, 1–4; H. Elaine Lindgren, *Land in Her Own Name* (Fargo: North Dakota Institute for Regional Studies, 1991), 73–74. The act was modified many times, including in 1912 when Congress changed the law to allow for a three-year, rather than a five-year, residency requirement. Lindgren notes that three categories of married women qualified for land under the Homestead Act—widows, divorcees, and, with adequate proof, separated or deserted wives with child dependents under the age of 18.

10. Olson and Naugle, *Nebraska*, 160; Schell, *South Dakota*, 168–69; J. Leonard Jennewein and Jane Boorman, eds., *Dakota Panorama* (Sioux Falls: Brevet Press, 1973), 137.

11. Jennewein and Boorman, *Panorama*, 113–45; Elwyn B. Robinson, *History of North Dakota* (Lincoln: University of Nebraska Press, 1966), 144.

12. Webb, *Great Plains*, 377.

13. O. H. Holt, *Dakota—Behold, I Show You a Delightsome Land* (1885), 12.

14. Jennewein and Boorman, *Panorama*, 224.

15. Olson and Naugle, *Nebraska*, 163–66; Schell, *South Dakota*, 175.

16. Schell, *South Dakota*, 122; Olson and Naugle, *Nebraska*, 88; Patricia Nelson Limerick, *The Legacy of Conquest—The Unbroken Past of the American West* (New York: W. W. Norton and Co., 1987), 197; Robinson, *North Dakota*, 134, 146, 246; Michael P. Malone, Richard B. Roeder, and William L. Lang, *Montana: A History of Two Centuries* (Seattle: University of Washington Press, 1991), 241–42. Schell notes that in the early 1870s in Dakota Territory, interest rates for real estate mortgages ran as high as 24 percent annually.

17. Nelson, *After the West*, 17–18.

18. W. E. Powell, General Immigration Agent, Chicago, Milwaukee and St. Paul Railway, *Dakota, the Land of Promise, How to Go and What to Do When You Get There* (Milwaukee: Riverside Printing Co., [n.d.]), 9.

19. Webb, *Great Plains*, 422–23; Nelson, *After the West*, xviii.

20. Robinson, *North Dakota*, 246.

21. Jennewein and Boorman, *Panorama*, 96.

22. U.S. Census Bureau, *Historical Population Counts*, http://www.census.gov/index.html, acc. Nov. 13, 2004; Peter Kilborn, "Bucking trend, they stay, held by family and friends," *New York Times*, Dec. 2, 2003; Glen Martin, "Where the buffalo roam, again humans are disappearing from Great Plains as bison and other wildlife return," *San Francisco Chronicle*, Apr. 22, 2001. For example, Fillmore County, Nebraska, had a population of 15,087 in 1900 and only 6,634 by 2000. Neighboring Clay County had a population of 15,735 in 1900 and less than half that (7,039) by 2000.

23. Kilborn, "Bucking trend."

24. James Shortridge, *The Middle West—Its Meaning in American Culture* (Lawrence: University Press of Kansas, 1989); Limerick, *Legacy of Conquest*, 29.

25. Schell, *South Dakota*, 175.

26. Schell, *South Dakota*, 175.

27. J. H. Carruth Misc. Collection, 1856 J1-0, Kansas State Historical Society (KSHS), Topeka.

28. Jennewein and Boorman, *Panorama*, 222.

29. Disaster Relief in Northwest Iowa, Records of Adjutant General, N51/03/06, State Historical Society of Iowa (SHSI), Des Moines; Schell, *South Dakota*, 88–89.

30. Merrill J. Mattes, *The Great Platte River Road* (Lincoln: University of Nebraska Press, 1987), 90. Mattes notes that "Indians . . . were aplenty, but as it often turned out, if left alone were unobtrusive."

31. Edward Nicholson Journal, MSS464, Colorado Historical Society (CHS), Denver; *The Democrat-Tribune* (Mineral Point, WI), July 22, 1971.

32. Lindgren, *Land in Her Name*, 224.

33. Small Manuscripts Collection, MSS20311, State Historical Society of North Dakota (SHSND), Bismarck.

34. Butcher Family Misc. Collection, 1871–90, KSHS.

35. Mary E. Lovell Carpenter and Family Correspondence, P1487, Minnesota Historical Society (MHS), St. Paul. A collection of Mary Carpenter's letters appeared in Sarah Brooks Sundberg's "A Farm Woman on the Minnesota Prairie: The Letters of Mary E. Carpenter," *Minnesota History* 51 (Spring 1989): 186–93.

36. Schell, *South Dakota*, 174.

37. Edward C. Kennedy Letters, H75-232, Box 3550A, South Dakota Historical Society (SDHS), Pierre.

38. Wilcomb E. Washburn, *The Assault on Indian Tribalism: The General Allotment Law (Dawes Act) of 1887* (Philadelphia: J. B. Lippincott Company, 1975), 18–21; Limerick, *Legacy of Conquest,* 198–99. In addition to the Five Civilized Tribes, the Dawes Act also initially exempted the Osage, Miami, Peoria, Sac, and Fox, the reservations of the Seneca Nation of New York, and a strip of territory in the State of Nebraska adjoining the Lakota Nation on the south.

39. Ann Fay Davis Collection, 83.238 Box 1, Folder 1, Oklahoma Historical Society (OHS), Oklahoma City.

40. Homestead National Monument of America, U.S. Department of Interior, National Park Service, http://www.nps.gov/home/homestead_act.html, acc. June 17, 2005.

41. Jennewein and Boorman, *Panorama,* 231.

42. Jennewein and Boorman, *Panorama,* 233.

43. Green Family Papers, MS4239 S1, Series 2, Folder 1, Nebraska State Historical Society (NSHS), Lincoln.

44. Uriah Oblinger Family Collection, RG1346.AM.S01.1103, NSHS.

45. M. K. Steen, "A Short History of a Pioneer in Traveling for Establishing a New Home," Feb. 15, 1938, Center for Western Studies Collection, Augustana College, Sioux Falls.

46. Williams Family Papers, H92-032, Box 5201A, SDHS.

47. Joseph Hall Collection, MSS 760, Box 1 FF 6, CHS.

48. Lottie Chesnut Papers, H95-030, Box 6033A, SDHS.

49. Arthur Joseph French Collection, P1621, MHS.

50. U.S. Department of Agriculture, National Agriculture Statistics Service, *2002 Census of Agriculture,* http://www.nass.usda.gov/census/, acc. Mar. 16, 2005; Thomas J. Marchione, U.S. Agency for International Development, *Foods Provided through U.S. Government Emergency Food Aid Programs: Policies and Customs Governing Their Formulation, Selection and Distribution,* American Society for Nutritional Sciences, 2002, http://www.nutrition.org/cgi/content/full/132/7/2104S, acc. June 15, 2005.

51. Schell, *South Dakota,* 176.

52. Schell, *South Dakota,* 177.

53. Schell, *South Dakota,* 177.

54. J. G. Towle Collection, H76.58, Box 3568A, SDHS.

55. Lewellyn Amos Gushee Collection, RG3972, Series 1, Folder 1, NSHS.

56. John Alfred Borg, Diary of a Swedish Immigrant, 1888–1899, RG0746, p. 96–97, NSHS.

57. U.S. Department of Interior, National Park Service, *Jefferson National Expansion Memorial—The Homestead Act of 1862,* http://www.nps.gov/jeff/homestead_act.html, acc. June 14, 2005.

58. Alice Newberry Collection, MSS 1202, Box 1, FF 24, CHS.

59. Artie and Ilma Cale Family Papers, 149I198F, Box 1, MHS.

60. Harlow A. Hyde, "Slow death in the Great Plains," *The Atlantic Online,* June 1997, http://www.theatlantic.com/issues/97jun/populat.htm, acc. Aug. 6, 2002.

61. Debra Marquart, "Between Earth and Sky," *New Letters: A Magazine of Writing & Art* 68 (2002): 35–51, http://www.lib.ndsu.nodak.edu/grhc/media/magazines/articles/marquart.html, acc. Oct. 5, 2003.

62. Robinson, *North Dakota,* 169–70.

63. Harriett Carr, MSS 107, FF 3, CHS.

64. Ella Bailey diary, MSS 28, FF 1, CHS.

65. Courtesy of Phyllis Sullivan, Daniel Sharp's youngest daughter.

66. Small Manuscripts Collection, MSS 20415, SHSND.

67. Western History Collection, CMSS-M284, SF3, Box 6, Denver Public Library (DPL).

68. Malone, Roeder, and Lang, *Montana*, 243.

69. Homestead National Monument of America, http://www.nps.gov/home/legacies.html, acc. May 2, 2003.

70. Ole Nilsen, the Younger, and Family Papers, P1229, Box 1, MHS.

71. Barbara Ault Family Collection, H88-5, SDHS.

72. MSS 404, H65-43, Wyoming Historical Society.

73. Susanne K. George, *Country School Legacy*, University of Nebraska at Kearney, http://platteriver.unk.edu/SchoolRoom.html, acc. Nov. 17, 2004. George notes that in 1871, 52 percent of Nebraska teachers were males.

74. Uriah Oblinger Family Collection, RG1346.AM.S01.1216, NSHS.

75. Edna Day Vardner, "Reminiscences of Homesteading near Mandan, North Dakota," 1961, MSS 20693, SHSND.

76. Nebraskastudies.org, *1900–1924 Native American Citizenship–1924 Indian Citizenship Act*, http://www.nebraskastudies.org/0700/stories/0701_0146.html, acc. June 6, 2005. In 1924, Congress passed the Indian Citizenship Act, granting citizenship to all American Indians born in the United States. Some states nonetheless prohibited American Indians from voting until after World War II.

77. Salina History Collection, 1861, July 7, KSHS.

78. Lulu Benjamin Letters, Small Collection 12, Montana Historical Society, Helena.

79. Smithsonian National Zoological Park, *American Bison—Thunder of the Plains Almost Silenced*, http://nationalzoo.si.edu/Support/AdoptSpecies/AnimalInfo/bison/default.cfm, acc. June 6, 2005.

80. Joseph Flick Collection, RG0999, NSHS.

81. Barbara Ault Family Letters, H88-005, Box 3751A, SDHS.

82. Small Manuscripts Collection, MSS 20064, SHSND.

83. Small Manuscripts Collection, MSS 20305, SHSND.

84. Lee W. Larson, *The Great Flood of 1993*, presented at the International Association of Hydrologic Sciences Conference, Anaheim, California, June 24–28, 1996, http://www.nwrfc.noaa.gov/floods/papers/oh_2/great.htm, acc. May 16, 2005; Federal Emergency Management Agency, FEMA News, "Colorado, Nebraska Hammered by Early-Season Blizzard," Oct. 27, 1997, http://www.hprcc.unl.edu/nebraska/oct97fema1.html, acc. June 16, 2005, and FEMA News, "Thousands Left Powerless Following Midwest Blizzard," Mar. 10, 1998, http://www.fema.gov/nwz98/wx0310.shtm, acc. June 16, 2005.

85. Nebraska Blue Book Online, 2004–2005 edition, "Nebraska: The Cornhusker State—General Information about Nebraska," http://www.unicam.state.ne.us/bluebook/intro/land_climate.pdf, acc. June 16, 2005; Nebraska Energy Office, 1999 Annual Report, Part I—Agency Activities, Energy Efficiency, Renewable Energy and Nuclear Waste Transportation Issues, http://www.neo.state.ne.us/AR1999/four.htm, acc. June 16, 2005; William A. Hayes and C. R. Fenster, *Understanding Wind Erosion and Its Control*, Cooperative Extension, Institute of Agriculture and Natural Resources, University of Nebraska–Lincoln, Mar. 1980, electronic version issued Aug. 1996, http://ianrpubs.unl.edu/soil/g474.htm, acc. June 5, 2005.

86. Sim Family Papers, Series 1, MS0278, NSHS.

87. Martha Janney Diaries, MS1110, p. 41–43, NSHS.

88. Mrs. Clifford Jencks Letter, H71-004, Box 3344A, SDHS.

89. Nelson, *After the West*, xxiii; Prairie Homestead National Historic Site, Philip, South Dakota, http://www.prairiehomestead.com/prairie_homestead.html, acc. June 20, 2005.

90. Diary, unknown author, SDHS.

91. Squire Lamb Collection, RG1561, NSHS.

92. Williams Family Papers, H92-032, Box 5021A, SDHS.

93. Shaw Family Letters, H87-014, Box 3748A, SDHS.

94. Edmund Morris, *The Rise of Theodore Roosevelt* (New York: Coward, McCann and Geoghegan, Inc., 1979), 373.

95. Reems Ranch Collection, MSS 1242, CHS.

96. Richard H. Steckel, *A History of the Standard of Living in the United States*, EH.Net Encyclopedia, edited by Robert Whaples. July 22, 2002, http://eh.net/encyclopedia/?article=steckel.standard.living.us, acc. Apr. 5, 2005.

97. Ellen Taber Collection, N20/8/5, box 4, SHSI.

98. Annie E. Casey Foundation, *Kids Count Indicator Brief—Reducing the Infant Mortality Rate*, July 2003, http://www.aecf.org/kidscount/indicator_briefs/infant_mortality.pdf, acc. Feb. 12, 2005; Edwin E. Graham, "Chairman's Address before the Section on Diseases of Children, at the Fifty-ninth Annual Session, American Medical Association, 1908," *Journal of the American Medical Association* 51(13): 1045–50, Sept. 26, 1908, http://www.neonatology.org/classics/graham.html, acc. June 8, 2005.

99. Ole Nilsen, the Younger, and Family Papers, P1229, Box 1, MHS.

100. Centers for Disease Control and Prevention Morbidity and Mortality Weekly Report, Aug. 13, 2004, *Epidemiology of Measles—United States, 2001–2003*, U.S. GPO, http://www.cdc.gov/mmwr/preview/mmwrhtml/mm5331a3.htm, acc. June 6, 2005.

101. Cotton Family Correspondence, H86-008, Box 3751B, SDHS.

102. Sim Family Papers—Series 1, MS0278, NSHS.

103. John M. Barry, *The Great Influenza—The Epic Story of the Deadliest Plague in History* (London: Penguin Books Ltd, 2005), 396–97.

104. Lulu Benjamin Letters, Small Collection 12, Montana Historical Society.

105. Olson and Naugle, *Nebraska*, 176.

106. *The Rocky Mountain Locust or Grasshopper, Report of proceedings of a conference of the Governors of several western states and territories, together with several gentlemen, held at Omaha, Nebraska, on the 25th and 26th days of October, 1876, to consider the locust problem* (St. Louis: R. P. Studley Company, 1876), 38–39.

107. Lisa Levitt Ryckman, "The Great Locust Mystery—Grasshoppers That Ate the West Became Extinct," *Rocky Mountain News*, June 22, 1999.

108. Jim Jones, "Grasshoppers: Life Cycle, Damage Assessment and Management Strategy," http://www1.agric.gov.ab.ca/$department/deptdocs.nsf/all/agdex3497, last updated Mar. 2002, acc. Nov. 14, 2004; Aaron Rieder, Doug Pascoe, Brad Evans, and Jason Phillips, "Grasshopper Plagues: Destitute Settlers," Southwest Missouri State College, http://ag.smsu.edu/Animal_Science/Grasshoppers/hopdesti.htm, acc. July 14, 2002; Aaron Rieder, Doug Pascoe, Brad Evans, and Jason Phillips, "Grasshopper Plagues: Were They All Bad?" http://ag.smsu.edu/Animal_Science/Grasshoppers/hoppeat.htm, acc. July 14, 2002.

109. *The Rocky Mountain Locust or Grasshopper*, 32.

110. U.S. Department of Interior, *Our Living Resources: A Report to the Nation on the Distribution, Abundance, and Health of U.S. Plants, Animals, and Ecosystems*,

Invertebrates/Grasshoppers, n.d., http://biology.usgs.gov/s+t/noframe/f074.htm, acc. July 12, 2002.

111. Cushman K. Davis, Governor's Papers, 111F54(F), MHS.

112. Schell, *South Dakota*, 120–21.

113. Disaster Relief in Northwest Iowa, Records of Adjutant General, N51/03/06, SHSI.

114. John William Gardiner Misc. Collection, 1875, JA1-D23, KSHS.

115. Rieder, Pascoe, Evans, and Phillips, "Grasshopper Plagues."

116. *8th Annual Report of the Missouri State Entomologist* (Missouri Department of Agriculture, 1875), 62.

117. David Christie and Family Papers, P1283, Box 1, MHS.

118. Jennewein and Boorman, *Panorama*, 234. The authors note that one-half of the original filers for free land claims in Dakota Territory deserted their claim before they could have taken title.

119. Paula Nelson's *The Prairie Winnows Out Its Own* (Iowa City: University of Iowa Press, 1996) provides an excellent in-depth account of the struggle faced by homesteaders and others in western South Dakota during the 1930s.

120. Disaster Relief in Northwest Iowa, Records of Adjutant General, N51/03/06, SHSI.

121. Ole Nilsen, the Younger, and Family Papers, P1229, Box 1, MHS.

122. April M. Washington, "Deerfield was founded on dryland near Greeley," *Rocky Mountain News*, Oct. 19, 1999, http://www.denver-rmn.com/millennium/1019stone.shtml, acc. Apr. 25, 2005.

123. Western History Collection, CMSS-M394, SF5, Box 9, DPL.

124. Williams Family Papers, H92-032, Box 5201A, SDHS.

125. Asa M. Wickizer Misc. Collection, Mar. 26,1875, KSHS.

126. Susan E. Offutt, "The Future of Farm Policy Analysis: A Household Perspective," *American Journal of Agricultural Economics* 84: 1189–1200, 2002, http://ssrn.com/abstract=368514.

127. Gitchel-Larsen Family Collection, RG3622, NSHS.

128. L. M. Stavig and Harold Torness Collection, 1881–1949, p. 106–25, Center for Western Studies, Augustana College.

129. Alice Newberry Collection, MSS 1202, box 1, FF 24, CHS.

130. Adeline E. Hicks Papers, Small Manuscripts Collection, MSS 20398, SHSND.

Montana claim shanty, about 1910

900 Miles from Nowhere was designed by Will Powers at the Minnesota Historical Society Press, and set in type by him and by Allan Johnson, Phoenix Type, Milan, Minnesota. The type is Miller Roman, designed by Matthew Carter. This book was printed by Thomson-Shore, Dexter, Michigan.